The Bullshit Factor

The Bullshit Factor

The Truth about
Corporate Disguises, Lies & Denial

James Bellini & Kati St Clair

♯

ARTESIAN

Every effort has been made to identify and acknowledge the sources of the material quoted throughout this book. The authors and publishers apologise for any errors or omissions and would be grateful to be notified of any corrections that should appear in any reprint or new edition.

Published by Artesian Publishing LLP
e-mail: info@artpub.co.uk
www.artpub.co.uk

ISBN 0 955 11640 6

Design and typeset by Surfbird Design

A CIP catalogue record for this book is available from the British Library.

CONTENTS

CASE STUDIES

EXHIBITS

ACKNOWLEDGEMENTS

We are eternally grateful for the continuing support and interest from friends and colleagues during the writing of this book. But our special thanks go to the following: Susanne Worsfold, Rose Alexander, Peter Gill and Elizabeth Sheinkman. The errors, omissions and conclusions, however, are ours alone.

Introduction

THE BULLSHIT FACTOR

The corporate universe is entering its third and most complex phase: the age of psychology-based management. In this new age the secret of business success will reside in the health and courage of the corporate psyche.

The first phase of corporate evolution stretched from the mid-19th century until the end of the Second World War in 1945 and was marked by the emergence of enterprises organised around relatively simple manufacturing production processes or the distribution of natural resources such as oil. They developed as 'industrial model' companies run by centralised command-and-control management systems similar to the military mind.

The second phase, from around 1945 until the end of the 20th century, saw the rise of a huge fraternity of multinational giants that have collectively become the dominant influence shaping the world economy and the texture of our everyday lives. Many were first-phase industrial model companies driven by aggressive new strategies for international expansion. But a great many others were new brands launched during the long post-war boom – brands that leveraged technologies and product innovations in an unprecedented way. Together these second-phase corporations have transformed the way we live, work and spend.

But over the later years of the 20th century there was also a parallel development that was to help create a new context for business and usher in a third phase of the corporate saga. People have changed. From mass markets of acquiescent and loyal consumers, attitudes have shifted towards a more individualistic outlook that calls on the corporate world to recognise and cater for their personal aspirational tastes – to engage with them in an increasingly customised way. In parallel with this there is now a growing focus by consumers on how businesses conduct themselves, on the idea of the 'likeable company'. Studies show that people want to work for, buy from and/or associate with organisations they respect, admire or identify with. Investment in ethical funds has soared, while consumers regularly punish big brands when their parent companies break the rules.

This trend has been reinforced by the epidemic of corporate wrongdoing that afflicted the business world as it entered the new millennium. It was personified by the Enron scandal and the related demise of Arthur Andersen, but the taint of fraud and greed has spread across the whole corporate landscape. As a consequence, regulatory authorities are now imposing rigorous standards on boardroom behaviour, with legal codes that impose million-dollar fines and send bosses to jail. For all these reasons, corporate conduct has now moved centre stage and honesty, truthfulness, transparency and fair dealing will be the watchwords for business leaders in the years ahead.

The third phase of corporate evolution is therefore about the personality traits that drive the actions of an enterprise – about the condition of its corporate psyche. How balanced and healthy is that psyche? Is it manifested in good conduct? And, of more pressing relevance to its survival and success, does that psyche support the future strategy and vision of the business? We will spell out in greater detail the key drivers of a healthy corporate psyche – and the various descriptors of a dysfunctional one. We will identify and explain seven psychological conditions that can be observed in the corporate community: *inertia, pessimism, timidity, frustration, aggression, arrogance* and *courage*. As with people, these psychological conditions have a direct bearing on an organisation's potential for achieving its future goals.

The marketplace of the 21st century will penalise companies that fail to address this new agenda. Just as important, it will penalise those companies that cover up, deliberately or unwittingly, underlying personality flaws and negative intent with an outer wrapper of cheesy, disingenuous conduct and hollow messages – with corporate 'bullshit'.

Companies that lie to themselves about who and what they really are – and hope their employees, customers, investors, suppliers and other stakeholders will not notice – may not survive for long.

It's All in the Corporate Mind

So it is time to change the way we analyse companies and the way they function. We need to move away from old-style management 'gurus' and strategists and adopt a new, hybrid discipline that blends professional psychology skills with marketplace savvy to gain valuable insights into why companies behave the way they do. The nature of this behaviour gives us vital clues as to the condition of a company's underlying psychological state and in doing so helps identify those companies that will succeed while others are doomed to fail. It also offers the means by which those companies confronting failure because of an ailing psyche can be given a new direction, towards revival and profitability.

The practical implications of this new approach are profound – truly revolutionary in how we look at the future of world business. The well-publicised collapse through scandal of leading companies like Enron, Arthur Andersen, Parmalat and WorldCom, the decline for other reasons of long established companies like Polaroid, Swissair and Pan Am and the ongoing commercial woes of leading brands like Philips, Levi Strauss, Sony and Marks & Spencer have all raised a blunt question: What went wrong? The superficial answers, of course, differ widely and range from criminal conspiracies and corporate greed to managerial incompetence or plain bad luck. But such case studies focus only on companies that have already fallen prey to some inner psychological weakness. Among the many thousands of companies operating in the global marketplace in a seemingly successful way, a surprisingly high percentage are unknowingly afflicted by personality disorders that could lead them, too, into business oblivion.

The Bullshit Factor is a radical departure from traditional thinking about business success. It is not about processes, products or clever marketing programmes. Nor is it about human brilliance in the boardroom. It is about the deep-rooted psyche of an enterprise that can only be found way beyond the actions of key executives, in a corporate persona invariably built up over many years.

In this sense it may be regarded as a pioneering book that will perhaps stir debate and disagreement. There is, of course, a small niche sector in management writing that looks at certain aspects of psychology in business. Manfred Kets de Vries, for instance, in his recent study, *The Leadership Mystique*,[1] examines the 'leadership factor' in corporations. As one reviewer observes:

> de Vries unpicks the many layers of complexity that underlie effective leadership and gets to the heart of the day-to-day behaviour of leading people in the human enterprise.

As those words confirm, de Vries goes no further than looking at the role of people in corporate behaviour. To get to the real truth you need to dig into the deepest levels of an organisation's psychological make-up and unravel its innermost personality traits by looking at what it says and does as an organisation and at the outer symbols it presents to the world around it as indicators of what is going on within.

There are also people in the psychology/law profession who address such issues as whether the corporation is a legal person and what roles and responsibilities it should adopt in helping create a better society. They touch on the possible connection between corporate psyche and business failure. One good example is Harry Levinson, who, in a paper, *Why The Behemoths Fell*,[2] published in 1994, attempts to unravel the reasons why large and previously successful organisations often experience difficulty adapting to significant changes in their marketplace. Levinson describes business organisations as 'living organisms' that have 'psychological verities'. Sometimes, he says, these verities create patterns of inertia that lead to missed business opportunities.

Levinson mentions two major examples of potentially fatal inertia that could be attributed to a form of corporate narcissism. One is General Motors' lethargy and inaction when confronted by early signs of powerful Japanese competition; GM simply stuck its corporate head in the sand. The other is IBM's failure to address the challenges of a shifting IT marketplace; it stayed rigidly attached to big commercial mainframe computers at a time when the frontiers of technology were being pushed back to make room for the desktop PC. In both cases their inaction had a serious impact on the bottom line. By the early 21st century, Toyota was three to four times more profitable than GM. In 2005 GM suffered a $10 billion loss and subsequently announced thousands of job cuts. In IBM's case the result was a descent into an $8 billion quarterly loss in 1993 that took years to reverse. In 2004 IBM sold its PC business to the Chinese – the equivalent of McDonald's selling off its burger business. It was part of a familiar pattern of corporate myopia for IBM: in the 1980s it hired a young college dropout called Bill Gates to develop an operating system for its PC range, but allowed Gates to hold on to the intellectual property rights of the system. IBM believed – wrongly – that the future of information technology would be firmly rooted in hardware, not software. Today the Microsoft Corporation Bill Gates founded ranks amongst the top 50 US companies; in 2005 it matched IBM's $8 billion annual profits.

The Icarus Paradox by Danny Miller,[3] published in 1990, follows a related theme. The book notes that great corporate success often precedes severe decline. Miller argues that the cause is a tendency for successful companies to continue backing their internal winners while depriving other innovative departments of the resources they need to generate the next phase of success. 'Very few organisations', he says, 'repair the roof when the sun is shining'. But both Levinson and Miller argue that the reasons for failure lie not in the embedded psychological traits of the organisation but in flawed relationships at managerial level. Levinson, for example, maintains that companies usually stumble because the chief executive was unable to take into account the psychological factors governing working relationships between his senior people. As we shall demonstrate, this is an important consideration, but is only part of the explanation as to why companies hit trouble. The main reason is invariably locked away in the overall psychological condition of the organisation itself. Our two examples of GM and IBM, for instance, represent cases of blocked vision that stemmed from a corporate psychosis developed over many years.

Another writer, William Bridges, has brought a generalist's mindset to the task, but, again, takes us no further forward. In *The Character of Organisations*,[4] Bridges follows a well-established route of attempting to categorise companies by use of a matrix of corporate descriptors adapted by Katherine Briggs and Isobel Myers from the work of Swiss psychologist Carl Jung. The Briggs–Myers matrix stresses characteristics of management style like extroversion and intuition (or their opposites) in driving a company's behaviour. But the result is a one-dimensional analytical tool that only addresses how a company's management might react to business challenges. It does not delve into the workings of the corporate psyche.

There is also the work of Robert Hare, an emeritus professor at the University of British Columbia, who has drawn on his knowledge of criminal psychology to develop a 'Psychopathy Checklist'.[5] Used primarily for making clinical diagnoses of psychopaths, this checklist has long been favoured by criminal investigators, including the FBI and British police authorities, to screen potential recruits. Similar methods are also used for the testing of teachers, fire-fighters and others in positions of trust. A psychopath, after all, is defined as someone 'with no conscience, a profound lack of empathy and a hypnotic charm that masks their true nature as pathological liars, master con artists and heartless manipulators'. Hare believes that the scandals that drove Enron, WorldCom and other corporations into bankruptcy could have been avoided if his analytical tools had been used to screen executives for psychopathic tendencies prior to their taking up roles that gave them access to billions of dollars.

But he, too, stops short of looking beyond individuals to the persona of the company itself.

The Bullshit Factor makes the journey beyond people, into the psyche of the corporation. Using a unique analytical approach, it applies the lessons of human psychology to the understanding of organisations. It scrutinises every aspect of corporate behaviour, not just a corporation's habits of conduct, but its outward manifestations: corporate logos, literature, advertising and marketing campaigns, statements from the Chairman or CEO, headquarters' architecture – in fact anything that expresses an organisation's 'corporate voice'. Its conclusions offer valuable insights into the hidden realities of today's business environment, of why companies behave the way they do, and how, to the trained eye, this conduct gives important clues about their psychological health and their chances of survival.

Understanding the psychological roots of any company's behaviour is vital to assessing its fitness for the future, whatever its size or the business sector in which it operates. The marketplace of this new millennium is very different from the mass markets that developed during the 20th century and created the disciplines of mass advertising and marketing. This new environment is being shaped by powerful trends in technology and social attitudes and the emergence of an 'aspirational consumerism' that puts the customer in charge. The rise of what we can call the 'Who am I?' marketplace – in which consumers see their buying decisions as acts of self-identification and personal expression – will demand changes in the way businesses sell their products and services and the channels they use to reach their customers.

People also think differently about what they expect of business organisations. Studies show that consumers now want companies to put good conduct at the top of their priorities and to focus on corporate transparency and good governance. Because of this shift in public thinking, commercial success now increasingly depends on achieving an ethos of clarity and truthfulness – qualities that reflect a company's psychological condition and which can only be found on the invisible side of the corporate balance sheet.

This book therefore poses a powerful challenge to traditional thinking about corporate practices and raises uncomfortable issues for every business decision-maker. What is a psychotic company? Why may such a company be doomed? What can be done to promote its psychological well-being? What is the secret of a healthy psyche? Can a company succeed if its psyche does not accord with its long-term commercial goals? Do dynamic leaders make any difference if the corporate psyche is out of sync? What mix of people and skills does a company need to support its psychological characteristics? What can we learn from analysing the psyche of successful enterprises – and that of those that have failed? Where are the possible corporate failures of the future? Many of these possible failures are today present amongst the ranks of the world's leading companies.

Corporate Disguises

The central theme of this book is that organisations present a personality to the world that is invariably misleading. It is misleading because it springs from some form of corporate self-delusion that prompts an organisation to lie to itself and others about what it truly is and does, in the same way that people may project the image they desire others to see instead of the one that reflects their true personality. For a business, the result is corporate bullshit – a corporate voice that sends out signals that do not match the underlying psychological realities. This mismatch can lead to flawed strategies, ambitions and beliefs, and ultimately to business difficulties and failure.

We explore the critical difference between a 'courageous' company and those beset by *inertia, pessimism* or *timidity* – 'passive' emotions that block their capacity to move forward through their depressive, negative impact. We also spell out the probable consequences for a business of being driven by the 'active' emotions of *frustration, aggression* and *arrogance,* which block vision by crowding out clear thinking with a jumble of misplaced ambitions. We contrast the power of corporate clarity with the negative energies that flow from corporate self-deception or warped perceptions about key realities. We unravel case studies of massive corporate denial that betray a deeply flawed underlying psyche. And we explore the personality characteristics that define a winning business.

Sceptical readers may think our theme is just another interesting, but passing, perspective on the business scene. They may believe it will soon go the way of other management theories that gather dust on the bookshelves of business schools and college libraries. In their time they were accepted as the Holy Grail for business leaders. And in time they have each given way to the next 'Big Idea' for managers. But this misses the point entirely. *The Bullshit Factor* is not a theory of management but a means of understanding the risks associated with a dysfunctional corporate psyche. We argue that only companies that have a clear, unambiguous, honest perception of what they are all about – a courageous persona – will be capable of managing for success in the long term.

In case the title of this book offends you, we would draw your attention to a recent essay by the respected American moral philosopher Harry G Frankfurt. In *On Bullshit,*[6] Frankfurt attempts to build a theory around the topic and in doing so makes a bold bid to define the spirit of the modern age. Bullshit, he observes, is an inevitable product of public life, 'where people are frequently impelled – whether by their own propensities or by the demands of others – to speak extensively about matters of which they are to some degree ignorant'. This observation will resonate through the pages that follow.

Frankfurt explores how bullshit is distinct from lying and argues that bullshitters misrepresent themselves to their audiences in a way that differs from liars. When people lie, he says, they deliberately make false claims about what is true. But they still have purchase on the idea of truth.

Bullshitters seek to convey a certain impression of themselves without being concerned about whether anything at all is true. Bullshitters are indifferent to the truth. Frankfurt concludes that although bullshit can take many innocent forms, excessive indulgence in it can eventually undermine the practitioner's capacity to tell the truth in a way that lying does not. Liars at least acknowledge that it matters what is true. And so, Frankfurt argues, bullshit is a greater enemy of the truth than lies are.

One explanation put forward for the pandemic of bullshit in the business world, on which this book reports, is the communications revolution of 24-hour rolling news and instantaneous information via the Internet. This revolution, runs the reasoning, has created an open-ended demand for comment and opinion and, frankly, there is just not enough 'truth' to go round. Brief reflection should, in fact, produce the opposite view, that this flood of information across global cyber-networks makes it more difficult to get away with fabrication.

The Bullshit Factor argues that the issue runs more deeply than this and is rooted in the inherent dynamic that impels corporations to succeed by any means, at any cost. And, in any case, bullshit has been around since people could talk. But, certainly, modern technologies may have presented us with a new danger. The preference of the 21st-century media for 20-second sound bites and glib buzz-phrases militates against hearing the more substantial arguments of specialists who lack the 'skills' of silver-tongued brevity and glossy performance so beloved of the broadcast networks. If this is true, we have handed over our lives – and our future – to the bullshit merchants.

Part One

THE COMPANIES WE KEEP

1

A PRESSURE TO DECEIVE

Corporation *n.* artificial person created by charter; an entity unto itself under the law.

The core argument of this book is very simple. Businesses behave like people: they have personalities and psyches. They behave like people partly because they are run by people and have invariably accumulated psychological heritage from the actions of people who have run them in the past. But over time organisations also take on personality traits of their own. They become, to use Harry Levinson's phrase, 'living organisms'. Some relatively young companies still bear the stamp of their founders. Others – GE, Nokia, Procter & Gamble, BP, Nestlé – are the product of many generations of leadership, each with its own distinctive characteristics and contribution to forming the persona of the organisation. But all have 'psychological verities' that shape their behaviour and determine their fitness for commercial success in the future. And almost all of them, young and old, have a propensity to indulge in corporate bullshit in one form or another.

Why does this matter? Quite simply, because bullshit blocks their chance of future progress as a business and may also make them destructive corporate citizens. On this citizenship issue alone, the verdict on corporate behaviour over the past century is far from encouraging. Enron, Parmalat, Global Crossing, Adelphia, WorldCom and a host of other billion-dollar corporate scandals are testament to this. Many such scandals resulted in the bankruptcy of the enterprise and huge financial costs that had to be borne by ordinary people through job losses, collapsing share prices and/or valueless pension funds. It is hardly surprising that a global public opinion survey in 2005 conducted by the World Economic Forum in 20 countries and covering more than 20,000 interviews revealed a deepening 'trust deficit'. The poll showed that trust in global companies stood at its lowest level since the survey's tracking exercise began.

We can read no better summary of the crisis in corporate trust than the words of David I. Greenberg, Chief Compliance Office of Altria Group, the parent company of cigarette-maker Philip Morris. Speaking at a conference in early 2005, he said: 'A few hours behind the glass wall watching normal people discuss their views of corporations and the executives who lead them will open a lot of eyes. We won't like what we hear and see. But it's a necessary, painful step toward getting corporate America back in line with society, and society with corporate America.'[1]

But the headline-grabbing corporate scandals are only part of the cause of this crisis of trust. The evidence points to a widespread erosion of the most basic standards of corporate conduct. One measure of this is the level of conflict between the corporate community and the law. Every year major business magazines publish annual lists ranking Big Business in America and around the world. There is the Fortune 500, Forbes 400, Forbes Platinum 100, the International 800 – and so on. They rank big corporations by sales, assets, profits, market share – even how much they are admired by their peers! Investigative analyst Russell Mokhiber has chosen a different task – to focus public attention on corporate criminality in the United States, a phenomenon that seems to afflict vast swathes of the business landscape. To compile his list he uses the most narrow and conservative of definitions: corporations that pleaded guilty or no contest to crimes and were criminally fined. While the cases are not necessarily about a lack of truthful behaviour, they offer an insight into the apparently cavalier attitude big corporations – US and otherwise – have adopted towards legal constraints on their conduct and their wider duty to the community, even though this can often involve colossal sums in court-imposed penalties.

To give a flavour of the sheer scale of this little-publicised battle between boardrooms and the courts, here is Mokhiber's round-up of the top ten corporate criminal convictions in US courts during the late 1990s. There are hundreds more. Note that non-US companies, doing business in the United States, feature prominently. Also be aware that the fines levied do not include the immense legal costs these companies would have incurred in pleading their case.

Company	Crime	Fine
1. Hoffmann-La Roche	Antitrust	**$500 million**
12 Corporate Crime Reporter, 21[1], (24 May 1999)		
2. Daiwa Bank	Financial	**$340 million**
10 Corporate Crime Reporter, 9[3], (4 March 1996)		
3. BASF	Antitrust	**$225 million**
12 Corporate Crime Reporter, 21[1], (24 May 1999)		
4. SGL Carbon	Antitrust	**$135 million**
12 Corporate Crime Reporter, 19[4], (10 May 1999)		
5. Exxon/Exxon Shipping	Environment	**$125 million**
5 Corporate Crime Reporter, 11[3], (18 March 1991)		
6. UCAR Int'l Inc.	Antitrust	**$110 million**
12 Corporate Crime Reporter, 15[6], (13 April 1998)		
7. Archer Daniels Midland	Antitrust	**$100 million**
10 Corporate Crime Reporter, 40[1], (21 October 1996)		
8. Banker's Trust	Financial	**$60 million**
12 Corporate Crime Reporter, 11[1], (15 March 1999)		
8. Sears Bankruptcy Recovery	Fraud	**$60 million**
13 Corporate Crime Reporter, 7[1], (15 February 1999)		
9. Haarman & Reimer	Antitrust	**$50 million**
11 Corporate Crime Reporter, 5[4], (3 February 1997)		

Source: Russell Mokhiber, Corporate Crime Reporter
www.corporatecrimereporter.com

Mokhiber is nevertheless keen to offer a few caveats. First, he says, big companies that have been criminally prosecuted in the United States are only the tip of a very large iceberg of corporate wrong-doing. There are many others that have not made it onto his lists, both those in the United States that have so far escaped prosecution and no doubt undiscovered corporate transgressors in other countries. Second, corporations can define the laws under which they live and do business. For example, he says, the US automobile industry over the past 30 years has worked overtime to block Congressional laws that would impose criminal sanctions in areas of auto safety. Auto companies, says Mokhiber, are still only subject in such areas to civil fines. Third, big corporations have immense resources with which to defend themselves in the courts of law and public opinion. Elsewhere in this book we have described the huge and costly legal efforts companies like ExxonMobil and Philip Morris have made to propound their version of the truth.

But, public disapproval of such behaviour apart, there is also the need to make companies fit for the future as wealth-creating enterprises. Every business decision-maker constantly asks the same question: 'Why do some companies succeed while others fail?' For years the business school gurus have told us that the answer lies in identifiable management processes, marketing strategies, innovation and new product development, and relationships with the customer. We depart from this traditional path and instead look at the underlying psychological realities that drive company behaviour.

Many will ask: Why attempt to understand the behavioural patterns of commercial enterprises? Is it not sufficient that they generate profits and create jobs? Why should we worry when a company misleads its marketplace – and itself – with false promises, fibs or fantasies? After all, a little bullshit never did any harm.

We beg to differ. Understanding the psychological make-up of companies is vital if two important goals are to be achieved. First, it is a means of isolating negative personality traits in an organisation so as to help its managers build a more successful enterprise. This alone is a major contribution to the common good. Successful companies create wealth and jobs, generate tax revenues for communal benefit and make important innovations. But with public trust in corporate institutions seriously eroded in recent years by a wave of corruption and greed, it can also help us to identify and treat those underlying factors that lead to the abuse of corporate power. Studies tell us the world's young citizens – the millennium generation – place healthy corporate conduct above growth and profits when considering the priorities they want to see in the running of commercial enterprises. And healthy corporate conduct springs from a healthy corporate mind.

So diagnosing the personality – the internal and external perception – of a company is a very necessary task. Finding and correcting dysfunctional elements can be a make or break affair for any enterprise. People wrongly see companies as abstract entities that have an independent life unrelated to their leadership, character and persona. As a result, most companies have very little or no awareness of the personality they express and the potential dysfunctions they encounter. This is storing up huge problems that could question their future survival. Equally necessary is the realisation that business appears to have grown and prospered over the centuries by protecting its true intentions with a bodyguard of lies. The principal lesson of corporate history seems to be that truth and profitability are uneasy bedfellows.

Exhibit: The Dishonest Truth about Business

We lie all the time and it wears us out. We manage our companies through a series of delusional clichés: 'The customer is always right,' 'I'm not angry,' and 'We're proceeding according to plan.' But lying takes a huge toll in terms of stress, anxiety, and depression.

– Brad Blanton, author of *Radical Honesty*

[Telling the truth] is a bizarre principle to apply to people, let alone to business, where holding back information or telling little white lies is par for the course. Managers, like politicians, have to be economical with the truth.

– Ruth Lea, one-time Director of Policy at the UK Institute of Directors, now Director of the Centre for Policy Studies

---

Lying lies at the heart of good business, but when all else fails, tell the truth.

– Michael Finley, co-author of *Why Change Doesn't Work*

If you have the right strategy and believe in what you are doing, you should be able to circumvent the need for anything but the truth.

– Julia Hobsbawm, British PR specialist and originator of the concept of 'Integrity PR', a topic explored in *Where The Truth Lies*, a book of essays edited by her.[2] Hobsbawm believes we need an institutional attack on the culture of spin and bullshit – nothing less than a 'truth institute': 'If I could wave a magic wand there would be a forum – part academic, part think tank. A place where moral philosophy is applied to the question of where information goes in the 21st century.'

One entrepreneur, Gerald Ratner, wiped out half a billion of shareholders' money and was forced to resign as chairman of Britain's largest high-street jewellers when truth got the better of him. At the Annual Conference of the UK's Institute of Directors, he revealed to delegates how he was able to peddle his trinkets at knockdown prices: 'Because it's crap.'

– *The European*, November 1997

Source: www.citypages.com/databank/19/894/article4194.asp

A short primer, 'When to Lie and How', if brought out in an attractive and not too expensive a form, would no doubt command a large sale and would prove of real practical service to many earnest and deep thinking people.

– Oscar Wilde in *The Decay of Lying*

The word 'psyche' comes from the Greek for 'soul' or 'spirit'. When applied to an organisation it refers to an inner personality that has formed over time – a collection of values, standards, habits and behaviours. If this soul or spirit is dysfunctional, in the sense of being out of balance with itself, commercial catastrophe may be not far away. Unless this imbalance is addressed and remedied, no amount of corporate bullshit – of self-deluding or misleading words or actions – can postpone the fateful day.

In its journey through the corporate psyche, *The Bullshit Factor* offers instructive insights into companies that are household names around the world – into why they behave the way they do and what their pattern of conduct tells us about their capacity for success in the future. It examines every aspect of a company's personality and how that personality is conveyed to others – through what it docs, what it says and what it projects visually to its many audiences. And it carries a blunt message for every enterprise: any company, even the best behaved and most honestly managed, can unknowingly fall victim to dysfunctional traits that undermine its ability to deal successfully with the changing pressures of the marketplace and hence place it in dire commercial peril.

But despite its enormous implications, this issue never makes it onto the boardroom agenda. One reason is that the broad majority of senior decision-makers just do not consider the health of their company's psyche; the topic is simply not regarded as a 'serious' component of sound business strategy. The second reason for ignoring potential danger signs is that those decision-makers believe that their organisation has an unwritten guarantee of long-term survival. Here, too, they are seriously misguided. Life in the corporate jungle can be nasty, brutish and short.

Business history tells us that the average lifespan of the modern corporation is little more than 30 years – about the same as a primitive hunter-gatherer hominid several thousand years ago. An instructive exercise is to chart the changes over time in the membership of stock market indices or corporate rankings published by business magazines. The churn of corporate names is surprisingly high, as winners and losers come and go.

- When the *Dow Jones* index was first put together in 1884 it contained just 11 names – nine railroads and two industrial companies. By the early 21st century what is now the Dow Jones Industrial Average had expanded to 30 corporations. None of those original 11 is among them.

- Check out the first *Forbes* list of the 100 biggest US companies, published in 1917. By the start of the 21st century only 18 of them still counted themselves among the country's 100 biggest. And only one – General Electric – had out-performed the market since that originating year.

- The *S&P 500* was first published in 1957. Of the original 500, only 125 still featured at the start of the third millennium; there has been an average of 20 additions and deletions each year since the list's inception.

- The original 1955 version of the *Fortune 500* list of leading US companies – the most prestigious list of all – also makes interesting reading. Although that first list included only industrial companies, it confirms the perilous nature of corporate life. Among the top 50 – the elite of US business at the time – were such names as Esmark, Wilson and ARMCO. Today, you could search the *1000* list and not find those names. Chrysler, then ranked sixth, disappeared from it altogether after being absorbed into Germany's Daimler Group in 1998. Other companies have plummeted from leaders to also-rans. Borden Chemical, then at number 33, has plunged to below 850; metals processor Ryerson Tull, then at number 49, is now not even in the top 500. On the other hand, Wal-Mart, today one of the world's biggest corporations, didn't even feature; the retail giant was not incorporated until 1969.

- Since the *Fortune 500* list was inaugurated in 1955, over 1800 US corporations have featured in it. Only 71 have been ranked in it every year. Much the same pattern of corporate mortality can be seen in Europe, Japan and elsewhere.

Analysts have traditionally explained this pattern of corporate decline and disappearance by pointing to practical causes – outdated products, uncompetitive prices, loss of market share to younger and more nimble rivals, poor customer service, cash-flow problems. But these are merely the external manifestations of failure, the outer symptoms of a yet undiscovered malaise. The true causes are linked to weaknesses buried in the psyche of the organisation that prevent it from taking appropriate courses of action to ensure future success: setting a realistic forward strategy, identifying and correcting operational weaknesses, adjusting to changes in the external competitive environment and/or seizing a new market opportunity.

The Emperor's Clothes

The reason any company fails to take such 'appropriate courses of action' is invariably because its vision is blocked by one or more inappropriate emotional states. By applying lessons of human psychology to corporate behaviour we can assess whether an enterprise lacks the clarity of vision needed to identify and pursue the route to future commercial success. The 21st century manager, in other words, needs to start thinking about the psychological drivers that shape the company's decisions and actions. Every corporate board, no matter what size the enterprise, should continually ask itself: 'What makes this organisation tick? Is its psyche "healthy" and fit for the demands of tomorrow's business challenges? Do its personality traits match its future vision? Or is it trapped in some dysfunctional emotional condition that clouds its outlook and hampers its chances of success?' If such an honest appraisal produces negative answers, it may be time to seek a fresh approach.

Such questions are never addressed in the steady flow of airport books spelling out the supposed business secrets of some corporate mogul or sharing 'Ten Easy Steps to Making a Million'. The work of commentators like Harry Levinson and Danny Miller, discussed previously, were exceptions whose analyses were, in any event, largely confined to professional debates and the business school circuit. But wider interest in the psychological characteristics of corporate behaviour has been heightened by the publication in 2004 of *The Corporation* by Joel Bakan.[3] The book was accompanied by a documentary film of the same name, shown across the world to considerable media attention. It featured campaigner Michael Moore, whistle-blowing TV journalists, 'corporate spies' and varied stories of corporate mis-behaviour, from callous bullion traders cashing in on 9/11 to case studies in massive environmental pollution and unethical marketing practices.

The central argument of *The Corporation* is that the modern corporation – certainly in its Anglo-Saxon form – is a 'person' that meets all the diagnostic criteria of a psychopath. In terms of human psychological stereotypes a psychopath has specific and distinct behavioural drivers marked by a single-minded, ruthless pursuit of chosen goals without any consideration for their impact on others. It is a stereotype that can apply to a murderer, a secret service assassin – or a corporation. This psychopathic character is largely the product of legal and cultural principles, developed over the years, that have given the corporation immense freedom to pursue profits and growth without any considerations beyond the interests of its shareholders. As Bakan puts it: 'The corporation's legally defined mandate is to pursue, relentlessly and without exception, its own self-interest, regardless of the often harmless consequences it might cause to others.' In this pursuit, the niceties of the law are sometimes expected to take a back seat.

Exhibit: Merchants of Truth?

There were exceptions to the narrow 'psychopathic' view of corporate mentality, especially in the early years of modern business history. In 18th and 19th century England, Quakers – religious dissenters who originally emerged in the mid-17th century – played a major role in the growth of many key business sectors, a fact attributed to their legal exclusion from other mainstream areas of public life. Quakers built the first-ever railway line, the so-called Quaker Line from Stockton to Darlington, in 1825. They founded the Lloyds and Barclays banking empires. Britain owes its early iron and steel industry to the Quaker Darby's of Coalbrookdale. Quakers were strong in brewing and even stronger in chocolate: Britain's four main chocolate makers – Cadbury, Fry, Rowntree and Terry – were all Quaker companies. Robert Ransome, a Quaker who in 1803 invented a plough that used interchangeable parts that could be replaced out in the fields, could rightfully be said to be the originator of production-line techniques later perfected by Henry Ford.

These Quaker entrepreneurs held strong religious convictions about reliance on trust and integrity in business. Truthfulness was a watchword; the sect's founder, George Fox, often referred to early Quaker groups as 'friends of the truth'. Their belief in egalitarianism ensured that women were given a fair share of managerial positions and that all employees were treated as equals. Cadbury even built a factory village at Bournville, near Birmingham, to provide his employees with affordable housing. It was highly appropriate that Sir Adrian Cadbury was commissioned in the early 1990s to produce a report on corporate governance for UK companies.

Many regard the Cadbury governance guidelines as the reason that Britain managed to avert a corporate collapse on the scale of Enron in the years thereafter. But by now this Quaker inheritance, with its strong moral drive, had long since diminished. Being privately owned family companies, vulnerable to takeover, Britain's Quaker companies have been steadily absorbed by bigger, non-Quaker corporations. Rowntree, for instance, which led the way in offering its employees a pension scheme, swimming pools and gymnasia, is now part of the Swiss food giant Nestlé. Rowntree's one-time Quaker rival, Terry, is now owned by a major Nestlé competitor, Kraft Foods, part of the Altria Group that owns cigarette-manufacturer Philip Morris. Barclays and Lloyds have been transformed into huge global banking concerns; Barclays is now ranked 14 in the world, with Lloyds at 21. The strongly ethical Quaker influence in shaping Britain's corporate personality has more or less disappeared.

The Corporation is certainly a useful starting point for analysing the psychological triggers of corporate behaviour. But it has two important shortcomings. First, it deals almost exclusively with US corporations and their failings as corporate citizens over the years. As we shall see, there are enormous differences in corporate cultures around the world and US experience is of limited relevance when analysing the psyche of, say, continental European or East Asian companies. Second, a psychopath is only one of a broad spectrum of psychological stereotypes and we have to consider them all if we are to tell the complete story.

What's in a Logo?

This book addresses that wider spectrum and presents, in uncomplicated language, a methodology for assessing the psychological state of an organisation. It produces a range of varied corporate types. It sets out a hierarchy of differing corporate psychological states and offers some simple tools for diagnosing the psychological 'truths' that invariably lie behind the outer shell of corporate logos, marketing messages, Chairman's statements, company literature and the rest – behind the corporate bullshit. And it identifies the bullshit-free psychological characteristics that are essential ingredients of a successful business formula. In a sentence: the less corporate bullshit, the more chance of survival, success and profitability.

By way of illustration, take the concept of the company logo. Everything about it has psychological relevance: its shape, visual references, size, colours, wording (logo comes from the Greek for word) – all convey some hidden meaning and help shape perceptions about the corporate brand for which it speaks. Throughout history, of course, shapes and symbols have exerted immeasurable influence over human thinking and behaviour – from the cross to the swastika. National flags hold thousands, even millions, in their thrall. Much of it springs from irrational or emotive impulses that all but defy explanation. Corporate branding draws from the same psychological well.

Small wonder companies may spend a fortune trying to create the ideal branding formula with a new corporate name or logo. Sadly for them, they often get it wrong. They also break an important business rule: tinkering with an established brand name is invariably a sign of some corporate personality disturbance and an early marker for difficulties ahead. For instance, when the consulting arm of accounting firm PricewaterhouseCoopers decided to rebrand itself in 2002 the cost of the exercise was put at £74 million. Unfortunately it decided to call itself Monday. Condemned by cynics for its overtones of inevitability and routine, senior management argued that the new name spoke of 'doughnuts, hot coffee and fresh thinking'. It mattered little; a few months later the firm was bought up by IBM and subsumed into its Global Services division.

Another telling example is Britain's Post Office, which traces its once-proud history back to its creation in 1635 during the reign of Charles I. In March 2001 the enterprise inexplicably decided to dump 360 years of heritage and recognition and change its name to Consignia, an action described by one branding specialist as 'a lesson in cultural destruction'. Confronted by a welter of public confusion and anger, as well as mounting hostility from the Post Office workforce, the business was forced to dump the offending brand name, suffering considerable cost and loss of reputation. In November 2002 Consignia became the Royal Mail Group. But a closer look at Post Office operations suggests that this damaging name-change exercise was an external manifestation of mounting problems beneath the surface. Around that time the business was rumoured to be losing around £1.5 million a day. More important, centuries of trust-based, world class service was, it seems, being massively eroded by a world class collapse in standards that can only be explained by the onset of a serious corporate personality disorder. In February 2006 the Royal Mail was fined £11.7 million by industry regulators for lost post and poor delivery performance. It emerged that 14.6 million letters, packets and parcels had been lost, stolen, damaged or interfered with during the previous year. It would seem that not only the mail had been lost: the disastrous re-branding initiative signalled an organisation that had lost both its confidence and its way.

Such examples merely serve to demonstrate the strange hold corporate logos can have over the consumer psyche and the dangers that lurk for those who interfere with them. But do they always speak the truth? In the same way that individuals send out signals – intentional or otherwise – through their choice of clothes, hairstyle and other aspects of appearance, a company hopes its chosen visual accoutrements strike the right chords with its various audiences. For this reason they are a rich vein of corporate psychoanalysis. Do they actually mean what they say? Is there harmony between what a company seeks to express through its symbolism and the underlying personality and behaviours of the enterprise? The degree of disharmony helps determine the degree of corporate bullshit.

Let us take one of the best-known logos of the modern age, the Nike 'swoosh' mark. It is widely regarded as an iconic symbol of the era of super-sports, with an almost religious association with energy and achievement. Consider this, quoted by author Naomi Klein in *No Logo*,[4] her radical reappraisal of the topic: 'I wake up every morning, jump in the shower, look down at the symbol, and that pumps me up for the day. It's to remind me every day what I have to do, which is: "Just Do It".' This mantra, she records, was voiced by a 24-year-old Internet entrepreneur about his decision to have the Nike logo tattooed on his navel. It could also be said that it carries an extra layer of meaning – the association with 'just do it' implies 'do not think or care – just do it!' It could be interpreted as a command for a total lack of empathy or conscience.

Klein goes further to scrutinise what lies behind the Nike logo. Her verdict is starkly contrary to the superficial impression of a company dedicated to harmless leisure and laughs. She describes a corporation obsessed with taking over not only the entire universe of sporting endeavour but the huge global business of sport as well: 'Nike, king of the superbrands, is like an inflated Pac-Man, so driven to consume it does so not out of malice but out of jaw-clenching reflex. It is ravenous by nature. It seems fitting that Nike's branding strategy involves an icon that looks like a check mark. Nike is checking off the spaces as it swallows them: superstores? Check. Hockey? Baseball? Soccer? Check. Check. Check. ... Tattoo parlours all over North America report that the swoosh has become their most popular item. Human branding? Check.' In later pages Klein chronicles the business practices of Nike – including allegations of sweatshop wages in its overseas factories – that have generated vast media coverage and growing anti-Nike activism. The issue she poses is central to the theme of this book: how much daylight is there between the company's projected image – what it wants us to think Nike stands for – and its everyday conduct as a business?

Similar observations can be made about the colours companies choose to clothe their corporate identity. Not surprisingly, corporate colours are carefully selected so as to encourage specific public perceptions about a company's personality, purpose and actions by appealing to various psychological triggers. Colour is energy and scientific experiments have proved that this energy has a psychological effect on us. Blind people have often been able to identify colours with their fingertips. Though there are only 11 basic colour words in English, there are many millions of colours. Each of those 11 basic colours has fundamental psychological properties, no matter what shade or tone is being used, and these properties can have either positive or negative output. At the heart of this colour universe are four psychological primary colours – red, blue, yellow and green. According to colour analysts, they relate respectively to the body, mind and emotions and to the essential balance between these three. Applied to the corporate world, this implies powerful psychological influences over how we judge a company, whatever the underlying realities.

Effective logos become synonymous with the organisations they portray. They are instantly recognised by millions of people and help to identify their companies and the combinations of symbol and colour scheme convey a message about the brands for which they stand. Sometimes the signals can be mixed and confusing, as in the case of IBM. Universally known as Big Blue – after its habit in the 1960s of delivering computing equipment in blue cases – its most favoured corporate logo is black and white.

Meanwhile, what conclusions are we to draw from the fact that BP, an oil company and therefore a target for environmentalists, has a logo shaped like a sunburst flower with petals in shades of yellow and green? Rumour has it that BP had its new logo wheeze checked out by a feng shui specialist before it was launched. What should we make of the decision of Altria, the owner of oft-maligned cigarette-manufacturer Philip Morris, to adopt a logo made up of multi-coloured squares? The company describes it as a 'mosaic symbol meant to convey the diversity that defines Altria's companies … and more ways to live up to our commitment to responsibility'. Cynics would say it is a sure sign the company is going through some kind of identity crisis. But whatever colour scheme a business decides to adopt in the interest of corporate re-invention and the need to project a new and dynamic personality, we should recall the words of one branding guru: 'When a business starts fiddling with its corporate colours, it is usually a sign it has lost the plot.'

Indeed, the task of choosing the right corporate colour is plagued with pitfalls. People associate different colours with certain feelings and emotions, but these associations vary according to culture and social or national traditions. What works as a positive and persuasive corporate messenger in one part of the world can backfire horribly elsewhere.

In most Western societies, for example, black is associated with death and is the colour of mourning. In India a recently bereaved widow may wear white, the colour most Western cultures associate with bridal wear. An Indian bride invariably wears red, while a dyed-in-the-wool Chinese communist sees red as the colour of revolution. What would either of them make of the bright lipstick red that adorns Ferrari sports cars and Ducatti motorcycles – both uncompromising symbols of red-blooded, capitalistic, macho sexuality? How would they react to the association of this same sexually charged colour with the word 'virgin' in Richard Branson's corporate empire? And would they be surprised that ExxonMobil, with its take-no-prisoners, big business ethos, made the same colour choice for its own logo? In the Far East business world, meanwhile, red suggests good luck – hence the bright red logos of Canon, Sharp and the Hong Kong and Shanghai Banking Corporation (HSBC). Coca-Cola is, of course, the grandfather of all corporate reds. Legend has it that Coke even gave Father Christmas his distinctive colour: the company's seasonal advertising in the 1930s reaffirmed the traditional image of a jolly fat man in a Coke-red outfit.

More specifically, red is a physical colour with connotations of courage, strength, masculinity, basic survival and excitement. Blue has an intellectual characteristic and is associated with intelligence, communication, trust, efficiency, logic and duty. Yellow has an emotional resonance and evokes optimism, confidence, self-esteem and emotional strength. Green is about balance and is most readily associated with harmony, universal love, reassurance and environmental awareness. It is not surprising that green was the enduring symbol of Body Shop for 30 years, despite what critics say about the company's true nature on matters of ecology. It is also highly revealing that in the revamped Body Shop, with its repositioning to appeal to affluent older women, the colour green has been relegated.

Perhaps that is a wise decision. Though it is painted as a benign colour linked to balance and universal love, green is in reality a ragbag of connotations and subconscious hints and should be used with care.

Regarded through the ages as the symbol of Nature, it was also in medieval times associated with demonic beings. Used in North American financial markets to signify rising share prices, in East Asian markets it is reserved for prices heading south. Redolent of the deprived emotion of envy – as in 'green with envy' and 'green-eyed monster' – it is at the same time connected to affluence, money, wealth and capitalism, epitomised in the US 'greenback'. It stands for inexperience – as in 'greenhorn' – but also for both 'fresh' and 'rotten' and even illness – as in 'green around the gills'. And aliens from outer space have long been depicted as 'little green men'. It also has strong political meaning in certain contexts; green is the adoptive colour of Islam and Arab nationalism as well as of Irish republicanism. Though green is the favoured choice of companies that want to trumpet their caring credentials, they should be wary. Green is the turncoat of colours that can suddenly stand the best intentions on their head.

The most popular logo colour is blue, with its connotations of truth, dignity, trust and reliability. Among blue's many corporate fans are Ford, Dell, Pepsi, Hewlett-Packard, Intel, Wal-Mart, Gillette, Barclays, Microsoft, General Motors, Procter & Gamble, British Telecom, Unilever and Deutsche Bank.

But perhaps the most interesting phenomenon in the universe of logo colours is the wide prevalence of companies that have chosen to use no colour at all. What can we conclude about logos based on black and white – or something in between? To be technical, black is all colours and the psychological implications of using it are complex and considerable. It absorbs energy coming towards it and enshrouds the personality it represents. On the other hand, in different ways white reflects the full force of the spectrum. Just as black is about 'total absorption', white is about 'total reflection'. Both colours are seen to have positive and negative associations, but corporations obviously hope to harness their beneficial attributes to put forward an attractive persona, even (or especially) when this disguises an unattractive underlying psyche.

Colour analysts ascribe many 'positive' values to these two 'non-colour colours' but are puzzled by the true characteristics of their close cousin, grey:

- **Black**: sophistication, efficiency, glamour, emotional safety, safety. Since it absorbs all energy coming towards it, black creates protective barriers. This 'colour' is in essence an absence of light because no wavelengths are reflected. Hence it can be menacing and has a ready association with fear and the unknown.

- **White**: sophistication (again), efficiency (again), hygiene, sterility, clarity, purity, cleanliness, simplicity. White also creates barriers, but they are different from those emanating from black. White screams 'do not touch me!' Like black, it is uncompromising. Visually, white can give an enlarged perception of space, though it can also make other colours stand out as garish, loud and unwelcome.

- **Grey**: this is possibly the most intriguing colour of all. Pure grey is regarded as the only colour that has no direct psychological properties. On the other hand, it is seen as being quite suppressive. When things turn grey we tend to curl up and resort to hibernation. Grey has a dampening effect and heavy use of it can indicate lack of confidence and fear of being caught out and exposed.

With references to fear, hibernation and the unknown, it may seem surprising that so many big corporate names have risked negative consequences to hide their selves – true or otherwise – behind logos or corporate identity colour schemes that draw on the palette of black/white/grey. Among them: IBM, BMW, Prada, L'Oreal, Playboy, Nestlé, Laura Ashley, Marks & Spencer, Apple, Adidas, Amazon.com and Ben & Jerry's.

So logos are useful gateways for any analysis of the corporate mind. The same can be said of other visual and physical trappings adopted by an organisation. A corporate HQ, for example, can project important clues about the personality of the company, its ambitions, self-perceptions, even dreams. Modern information technologies have transformed the administrative processes of organisations, allowing large enterprises to be managed through networks and extended communications systems. Increasing numbers of companies have trimmed back their HQ headcount and downsized to modest accommodation, pushing managerial self-rule out to the corporate equivalent of 'the colonies'. The idea of a huge trophy building acting as a centralised head office, so typical of old-style corporations, has become largely outdated. Interestingly, many such trophy buildings still lie dotted across the business landscape – edifices of a corporate personality clinging to a glorious heritage or the grandiose visions of its illustrious founder.

Case Study: What's in a Building?

In the small Texas town of Plano, a few miles north of Dallas, the curious traveller comes upon the massive HQ complex of EDS. Founded in 1962 as Electronic Data Systems by the diminutive Ross Perot, the company grew into a colossus among the first wave of information-age corporations. Forty years later EDS was employing over 130,000 people in 60 countries. Its annual revenues exceed $22 billion, more than the GNP of most African countries. The company is closely inter-linked with the Texas business elite headed by the Bush family. Its board of directors is graced by the likes of James A. Baker, III, Secretary of State under George Bush senior at the time of the first Gulf War. EDS has close business connections with the US military; in 2000 it was awarded the largest-ever federal IT contract in US government history – a $6.9 billion project for the Navy/Marine Corps.

By then the EDS story had moved on. Perot sold EDS to General Motors in 1984 for $2.5 billion and the company was subsumed into the vast infrastructure of the automotive giant. But how much of Perot's unique personality had rubbed off on the organisation and helped shape the design of the Pentagon-like headquarters the company has occupied since 1993? Certainly, the colourful Perot projected a personality of epic scale – the very embodiment of the idealised US business dream. From humble beginnings – Perot grew up in the Great Depression – he attained billionaire status by backing a timely commercial idea with sheer force of will. EDS, which he started with $1000, is credited with having invented the systems integration industry.

Perot says he learnt his approach to leadership at the US Naval Academy, a militaristic heritage that is stamped all over his career. For years Perot's office door carried a sign saying: 'Every Good and Excellent Thing Stands Moment by Moment on the Razor's Edge of Danger and Must Be Fought For'. A leading entrepreneurial publication described him as 'America's quintessential cowboy capitalist'. Running a fledgling business was never enough; he seemed to want everything. If he was not organising a secret mission to free two EDS employees from an Iranian jail in 1979 (the inspiration for the best-selling novel *On Wings of Eagles*) or attempting to fly supplies to US prisoners of war in Vietnam, he was buying a slot in US cultural history. He paid $1.5 million for a copy of Britain's Magna Carta and then donated it to the US National Archives.

As for the Plano HQ, it expresses the same mix of military, derring-do outlook and a flamboyant 'I-want-it-all' psyche. Some observers would say the Plano complex strongly reflects the psychological traits of the company's founder, that it displays a megalomaniac ethos based on Perot's own character. The company itself could be said to come across as arrogant, aggressive and over-presumptuous. One journalist who visited Plano whilst preparing an industry story summed up the feeling: 'The EDS campus is vast ... not unlike something out of a James Bond movie ... All this reinforced that EDS is big, very big'.[5]

This HQ says several things. 'I'm bigger than everyone else. I'm more secretive. I'm hidden, so you cannot find me and I know all your secrets. Anything you throw at me I can handle'. This building is rather like a well-defended castle, with a touch of Stalin's social-realist architecture. Although Ross Perot is no longer with the company, its HQ displays something of the megalomaniac ethos that observers have attached to the man himself.

> When pressed in an interview as to why he decided to sell out to GM, Perot replied: 'You can go back to the Bible ... Man, when he is successful for too long, becomes arrogant.' Somehow this piece of Perot wisdom never reached the architect who designed Plano.

Just as critical is analysing how a company communicates to itself and to the outside world. Language – the vocabulary, style and tone of a person's speech – is a valuable window into that person's innermost psychological realities. The same applies to the words deployed by a company to spread its messages. Ironically, corporate language is one of the greatest barriers to understanding in the world of business. One concerned consulting firm has even spent time and money developing a new software program, The Bullfighter, to sift the bullshit from company reports. Significantly, its consultants discovered a direct correlation between an overdose of jargon and poor corporate performance. When they tested out the program on the Enron accounts they noted a tendency for the language to become increasingly obscure as the company slipped towards financial disaster. A study of the top 30 US corporations, meanwhile, has found a clear tendency to use gobbledegook to disguise shrinking profits.

Plain language is now an avowed goal of many forward-looking organisations. But most still rely on the power of over-complicated language to disguise reality, defend entrenched political interests and – most crucially – prevent clarity. Thereby they strengthen the belief that the best way of communicating is by lying or confusing. Often it is used deliberately to defeat clarity so as to generate and protect personal power within a hierarchy. At other times it is deployed to add a spurious authority and gravitas to simple points. Or it can be used to bewilder – and thereby control – customers and even employees. And then there is marketing-speak, the language of a culture where words are woven into the most elaborate confections. Consider this extract from a speech in New York in November 2005 by Louis C. Camilleri, Chairman and Chief Executive of cigarette-maker Altria, celebrating the company's burgeoning success: 'Philip Morris USA has achieved significant growth for Marlboro by providing adult smokers with a preferred value equation comprising product, packaging and price.' Granted, it sounds more impressive than 'people seem to like our ciggies'. Readers keen to escape the clutches of the marketing-speak virus could do worse than read William Strunk and E. B. White's classic book *The Elements of Style*.[6] First published in 1918 and running to just a hundred or so pages, it should be force-fed to budding marketers at birth.

As with people, dysfunctional psychological conditions have a direct bearing on an organisation's potential for achieving its future goals. In later chapters we will apply these and other analytical tools to the examination of case studies from around the world of business. We will unravel the underlying psychological reasons for the continuing success (so far) of global enterprises like – say – General Electric and British Petroleum (or BP, as it now prefers to be called in the hope of escaping awkward connections to the negative environmental connotations of the oil business). We will consider the failure of once-eminent companies like Marconi, the criminal conduct that led to the collapse of corporations like Enron and Parmalat and the commercial woes of world brands like Levi Strauss and Sony. Alongside these corporate giants we will briefly focus our gaze on some small, young companies that could – given a healthy psyche – become the new leaders in years to come.

Exhibit: Online Bullshit!

For those who have neither the time nor sufficient love of tarradiddle to concoct ornate phrases of corporate deception, help is at hand courtesy of the Internet. If you enter 'corporate bullshit' in the Google search engine, for example, you will be directed to over 1,700,000 pages. A more failsafe method is to check out The Corporate Bullshit Generator for a free and never-ending supply of meaningless linguistic flimflam guaranteed to impress any senior work colleague or prospective employer blessed with a room-temperature IQ. Here is a brief selection of action-orientated marketing-speak:

'facilitate integrated markets'

'implement high-end architecture'

'transform ubiquitous infrastructures'

'orchestrate user-centric content'

'streamline robust initiatives'

'empower mission-critical deliverables'

'expedite enterprising methodologies'

'engage holistic systems'.

For more, visit: www.members.aol.com/matt999/bullshit.htm.

Enter the Gurus

Far from being a whacky, New Age route to understanding 21st century business, the idea of examining the corporate psyche – and the behaviours it may produce – has impeccable credentials stretching back to the early years of the industrial era. A hundred or so years ago a pioneering breed of academic writers, including Mary Parker Follett, Elton Mayo and Lillian Gilbreth, endeavoured to unlock the psychological dimensions of business organisations. The coming of the railways and other large-scale commercial entities in the 19th century had excited growing interest in how organisations function and evolve. A new academic discipline of organisation behaviour emerged. Gilbreth's *Psychology of Management*,[7] published in 1914, was among the first works that overtly expressed the idea that organisations have behaviours and that, contrary to the received wisdom of her day, those behaviours are invariably neither rational nor utilitarian.

But this line of thinking never developed into a front-rank school of analysis; nor did it take hold at the heart of management thought. It would be largely deployed in the practical pursuit of greater organisational efficiency through work simplification, improved production processes and the creation of more motivating working conditions. The technique of time-and-motion studies is probably its most lasting legacy. The idea of a 'corporate psyche', though latent in the work of Gilbreth and others, was consigned to the footnotes of business study. As the 20th century progressed, the emphasis switched to a focus on the role of 'management' as a profession and the strategies they might devise, and those pioneering steps into business psychology took a back seat.

By mid-century the energies of management writers were being applied almost exclusively to the means of increasing the productive capabilities of the corporate enterprise. This challenge was given increased urgency with the defeat of Hitler in 1945 and the onset of a Cold War against a feared Soviet communist enemy – a war that would be waged, as it happens, chiefly through economic confrontation and measured by comparisons of productivity, GNP growth and relative living standards. In 1946 Peter F. Drucker published *Concept of the Corporation*;[8] he thereafter became the unchallenged doyen of management writers for two generations. He pointed to companies like General Motors as models of the wealth-creating superiority of the capitalist corporation compared to its lethargic, state-run, centrally-planned communist competitors. He described the corporation as 'the representative institution of American society' and stressed the role of efficient production-line techniques, innovation and managerial commitment in maximising output, profits and jobs.

Drucker's book thereby defined the core characteristics of the second phase of corporate evolution – the corporation as a single-minded, super-productive entity geared to aggressive growth, market domination, the pursuit of popular abundance and the defeat of a communist economic machine. Indeed, a major factor stimulating the aggressive growth of Western corporate power after 1945 was the relative stability of the international economy produced by that same Cold War stand-off. In the end, the Soviet Union and its client states in eastern Europe would disintegrate under the weight of their in-built economic inefficiencies. The true victors of the Cold War were to be found not in the Pentagon or the White House but in the boardrooms of corporate America.

Drucker did not touch, back then, on the psychological considerations so critical to commercial success in this third phase of the corporate saga. He nevertheless raised an issue of enormous relevance to the subject matter of this book. 'The central problem of all modern society', he wrote in 1946, 'is not whether we want Big Business but what we want of it, and what organisation of Big Business and of the society it serves is best equipped to realise our wishes and demands.' Over half a century later this issue is more live – and more in need of resolution – than ever it was in the gloomy aftermath of the Second World War. What people want of 'Big Business' today, it seems, is a commitment to ethically sound business practices built around a wholesome corporate psyche. Put another way: make money by all means, but do it through responsible and truthful behaviours.

And here we encounter the central proposition of *The Bullshit Factor*. This popular desire for honest and responsible companies is contrary to the subconscious imperative that shaped the behaviour of Drucker's Big Business corporation, for his was an organisation whose 'superiority' was built on an inherent disregard for truth and the morals of the con-man. That imperative has had no better summary than in a paper published in the esteemed *Harvard Business Review* in 1968, the same year students were rampaging through campuses across Europe and North America to express their outrage against the capitalist order. In '*Is Business Bluffing Ethical?*' author Albert Z. Carr set out the case for corporate deception: 'The pressure to deceive is felt everywhere in business and deceptions are ethically justifiable … departing from the strict truth and the golden rule is part of the strategy of business.'[9] As this book will demonstrate, corporate boardrooms took to this idea with great enthusiasm. After all, they had been following it for years. It still drives the conduct of most companies, even in this allegedly enlightened and transparent age.

2

GREATER THAN EMPIRES

Whatever the political currents running through his book, Peter Drucker was writing at a seminal time, on the eve of corporate imperialism. In the 1940s the world economy was on the brink of what author Bruce Brown[1] has termed the Second Dominion of the Corporation – a vast explosion of business organisations in every corner of human activity from banking and car-making to healthcare, clothing, entertainment, travel, retailing, pharmaceuticals and law. Over the ensuing half-century this second coming would revolutionise the global wealth-creating machine and usher in an era of corporate supremacy that has totally reshaped the world economy and – to echo Drucker's prescient comment – raised urgent questions about exactly what kind of Big Business we want. For so many corporations deceit and lack of regard for truth and the golden rule became everyday practices on the road to great wealth and corporate stardom.

A curious aspect of this Second Dominion is how little attention we have paid to its nature, scale and consequences. As citizens we have, for generations, taken great interest in major political and economic developments, in issues of war and peace, and poverty and prosperity. But we have largely ignored the evolution of corporate history even though, as Brown reminds us, the idea of the corporation is many centuries old and most elements of modern corporate life are actually artefacts of the ancient past. As a result of our indifference we have never developed a coherent view about where the corporation fits into our social order or sought to understand the intangible factors that drive its behaviour.

During its 1500-year journey the corporate concept has developed from obscure religious beginnings to its current status as the most influential institution of the 21st century. Along that journey it has continuously mutated in form and its underlying psychological foundations have changed with it. Differing social and cultural influences have created a mosaic of corporate types across the globe. Small ventures, moulded invariably by a single individual, have evolved over decades into huge, multi-billion-dollar enterprises run by cohorts of men and women in suits. Recent years have seen the emergence of a hybrid of the two – rapid-growth corporate giants like Microsoft, Virgin and Dell that have attained global scale with their founder-leader still in charge. But whatever their origins, geographical location and special individual characteristics, they present a major challenge of understanding and appraisal. What exactly is 'the corporation' all about?

The word comes from the Latin *corporæ*, meaning 'to physically embody'. The oldest surviving example of a corporation is the Benedictine Order of the Catholic Church, founded in AD 529. The first corporate convention ever recorded was held by Cistercian monks in the early 12th century. The trousers worn by today's thrusting corporate executive are derived from the 16th-century attire of Venetian *corporados*, who adopted this dress code from the Muslim Orient – a wry twist given the opposition of strict Islam to so many capitalistic business practices. The Catholic origins of the corporate idea, meanwhile, have great relevance in the modern age. The Vatican is now the heart of a vast financial and managerial undertaking, though one seemingly beset these days with its own special brand of business challenges.

Case Study: Vatican Inc.[2]

Apart from being the spiritual focus for its faithful, the Catholic Church is also a giant business. With over a billion customers, many thousands of employees across the world and a vast property portfolio on five continents, this 2000-year-old enterprise is the equal of any global company. But, as *Business Week* has reported, despite massive growth in its customer base under the recently deceased Pope – under the pontificate of John Paul II the number of Catholics increased by 40 per cent to 1.1 billion – the Catholic Church faces growing problems.

First, the Church is desperately short of staff. In the US in the 1950s there was one priest for every 650 parishioners. Today the ratio is one to 1500. The average age of US priests is 60. In Europe the picture is similar. In Africa, Latin America and Asia the number of priests is growing, but not quickly enough to keep pace with exploding Church membership. In Latin America the priest ratio is one to 7000. In remote areas, people are lucky if they see a Church employee once a year. Other areas, such as Africa, lack the funds to build seminaries that can train new priests.

This is creating a serious crisis in customer relations, since the core customer service activity of the Church, the liturgy of turning wine and bread into the body and blood of Christ, can only be performed by a priest. The danger here, say religious commentators, is that as the Eucharist becomes less available to its members, Catholicism will be transformed from a sacramental faith into more of a word-based faith – just like its Protestant rivals. Indeed, it is reported that in South America millions have defected to Protestant ways of worship over recent decades. One reason, it is said, is the more welcoming atmosphere of Protestant congregations, which are noted for their closer relationships and less hierarchy. Many also point to the huge and growing gap between what the Catholic Church demands of its customers and what modern consumers actually want. While many Latin Americans embrace Catholic traditions of prayer and religious holidays, they ignore teachings on divorce, birth control and homosexuality – a powerful example of a corporate mission statement that has been left seriously behind by the changing dynamics of the company's marketplace.

One solution to this staff shortage might be the radical step of abandoning the rule of priestly celibacy. This would be the equivalent of Ford Motor Company moving out of manufacturing cars.

Second, there are the company accounts. Although the popular belief is that Rome controls considerable wealth, nobody knows how much money the Catholic Church raises and spends each year or any details of its budgeting. But it is no secret that a recent sexual abuse scandal in the United States cost the Church around $700 million and reduced the flow of collection revenues from disillusioned parishioners. The financial situation there was already delicate: US Catholics donate only 1.1 per cent of their income to the Church, half the level for Protestants. In places like Africa local dioceses don't even raise enough money to cover basic operating expenses, never mind helping the needy.

In all of this, much criticism is focused on the legendary lack of transparency that surrounds Church activities, especially its finances. Catholic reformers, including senior bankers like Geoffrey Boisi, former Vice-Chairman of JPMorgan Chase, have called for dioceses to publish an annual budget and a strategic plan so that parishioners can see where the company's money goes. They also argue that ending secrecy on financial matters would encourage Church members to increase their contributions. Others recommend splitting the Church's management structure into two, with administrative functions outsourced to a professional outside organisation able to give an improved level of public accounting and disclosure.

And third, there's the management. The late John Paul II brought more and more power back into the Vatican – creating the corporate equivalent of an old industrial model company run by an invisible autarky barricaded on the top floor of corporate HQ. So the company's senior executives – cardinals and bishops – got to see the boss maybe every three to five years. At General Electric during his reign, Jack Welch spoke to his top people every day. As a result of this highly centralised Church structure, problems in more distant parts of the business invariably pass unnoticed by the top brass. Reformers cite the US sexual abuse scandal as an inevitable result and say Rome should borrow 'best practice' from successful multinationals. Vatican supporters reject this line. They say that just as there was only one Christ, there must be only one CEO, with sole authority.

Compared to those early religious orders, business corporations are relative late-comers. The oldest surviving business corporation is probably Sweden's Stora Kopperberg, established in 1288 and now known as StoraEnso. But for centuries thereafter, incorporated entities remained a rarity. When the early roots of modern business did take hold there were more scams and scandals than honestly constructed commercial projects. Late 17th-century London, for example, was teeming with dubious characters trying to dupe investors into backing equally dubious corporate schemes. It culminated in the infamous South Sea Bubble, which cost many fortunes and even lives before Britain's Parliament, in an effort to stem a rising tide of fraud, outlawed the very concept of incorporation.

It would be some time before the corporation regained a semblance of respectability and the legal right to do business. The United States, for instance, is today regarded as the homeland of corporate culture. But at the time of her independence in 1776 the country possessed only seven chartered business corporations. And though this number was to increase significantly in the years that immediately followed (the headcount of US corporations grew tenfold between 1781 and 1790), it would be many decades until the birth of a few fledgling enterprises on both sides of the Atlantic. At the dawn of the 20th century most of today's mega-brands had not even been invented. The mighty Ford Motor Company – perhaps the defining corporate entity of the industrial age – was incorporated in 1903, with an investment of $28,000. The first Kellogg's cornflakes rolled off the bakery production lines in 1906. IBM was established in 1911, BMW in 1913, Boeing in 1916 and VW in the 1930s. Hewlett-Packard was started in a Palo Alto garage in 1939, as the first gunfire of the Second World War two rolled across Europe. But the floodgates of corporate expansion were about to burst open and the balance of economic power in our world would never be the same again.

Post-War Big Bang

Empires, nation states and political leaders played an important part in shaping the 20th century, but they would soon be dwarfed by the rapid rise of the Big Business enterprise – a phenomenon without precedent in history. In the space of a few decades the corporation emerged from nowhere to become the dominant institution in global affairs, wielding greater influence than governments or religions, taking hold of our social aspirations, redrawing our natural environment and driving the agenda of everyday life. Historians will judge the 20th the corporate century – the pinnacle of boardroom power, when corporate wealth and actions went largely unchallenged .

The collective economic might of these corporate colossi has become awesome, overshadowing nation states and even entire continents. At the dawn of this third millennium the combined market value of the top 500 US companies exceeded $10 trillion – ten times greater than all the economies of Africa and the Middle East put together. Just one of those companies – the mega-retailer Wal-Mart – generates more revenue each year than the whole of Austria, which makes Wal-Mart the twentieth biggest economic power on Earth. This is a remarkable feat for a business that did not even exist in 1960.

And not just in North America. The top ten European corporations now boast combined annual revenues of more than $1.2 trillion; the top 50 turn over nearly $4 trillion. The ten biggest Japanese corporations together represent over $750 billion in annual sales. South Korea's top four companies add up to $155 billion – bigger than the gross national product of Portugal. And China is now joining their ranks: in 2005 her five biggest corporations had total revenues in excess of $150 billion and they are growing fast.

Over recent years certain business sectors have seen steady consolidation through mergers and acquisitions, especially oil, banking, cars, food manufacturing, retailing and pharmaceuticals. The result is a new category of super-corporations so powerful that they can dictate the rules of the international economy. As one British newspaper has put it: 'There were times not long ago when drug companies were merely the size of nations. Now, after a frenzied two-year period of pharmaceutical mega-mergers, they are behemoths which outweigh entire continents. The combined worth of the world's top five drug companies is twice the combined GNP of all sub-Saharan Africa and their influence on the rules of world trade is many times stronger because they can bring their wealth to bear directly on the levers of western power.'[3]

But the immense financial presence of the world's corporate enterprises is only part of the story. Of equal importance is the speed with which they built that presence, leaving legislators, regulators and public opinion constantly playing catch-up in setting rules governing corporate behaviour. To be more accurate we should really talk of a corporate half-century, since the real take-off in corporate power and reach is a feature of the period following the Second World War. Some were companies with 19th-century roots that were swept along by the massive post-1945 growth in global trade, investment and prosperity. Others were totally new enterprises launched on the back of a wave of new technologies and product innovations. Most of these new arrivals possessed a mindset very different from that of their more senior counterparts, which by now were three or more generations old with a long legacy of accumulated personality traits. But all of them, young and old, have one thing in common. They all have an inherent psychological 'soul or spirit' that shapes their business actions. And some have more than their fair share of whimsy, even insanity, in their corporate history.

Mixing the Corporate Cocktail

The older Anglo-Saxon enterprises – the likes of Heinz, Procter & Gamble and Unilever – offer a particularly interesting perspective on the notion of corporate psychology. As case studies, they began as small pioneering ventures, often founded on the mental drive, idiosyncrasies or eccentricities of visionary individuals. In some cases there was even a touch of madness that eventually carried them way beyond the boundaries of their business into some kind of nutty twilight world.

Exhibit: Bonkers Bosses

Business history has more than a sprinkling of corporate Titans afflicted by quirky traits, eccentricities or mental instability. Is a warped mentality a common bedfellow of boardroom success and vast wealth? It is recorded that the oil billionaire **John Paul Getty** – his father was reputedly the world's richest man -- installed pay telephones in the guest rooms at his sumptuous Sussex mansion. And that his son, a generous benefactor who once gave £100,000 to Britain's striking coal miners, died a recluse in the British capital. Another wealthy oil magnate, **Nubar Gulbenkian**, drove round 1960s London in an antique Rolls Royce-built taxi complete with coach lamps. 'It turns on a sixpence', he once said, 'whatever that may be.' It is said that for **William Lever**, founder of the Lever Brothers soap business that eventually became Unilever, a cold winter's day at his palatial Lancashire estate would start with him cracking the ice on the surface of his outside bath before taking to the more-than-bracing waters.

Such eccentrics are harmless in their way and quite different from more sinister versions of the barmy tycoon.

Howard Hughes, in contrast, spent his later life steeped in bizarre habits: cutting his nails once a year, sitting naked on a white leather chair in a 'germ-free zone' and using Kleenex boxes for shoes in locked-down, blacked out hotel penthouses surrounded by Mormons. Hughes, who inherited his father's oil-drilling fortune in 1924, when just 18, cut a swathe through southern California's two glamour industries of movies and aviation. He built a vast wealth-producing machine embracing three airlines, an aircraft company, a movie studio, a tool company, casinos and hotels in Las Vegas, a medical research institute and enormous real estate interests. But the wealth and power – and perhaps a youthful encounter with syphilis – got the better of him. Hughes – later to become the central character in the Hollywood movie 'The Aviator' – had two nervous breakdowns and took to drug abuse. He became an itinerant recluse, transporting a huge caravanserai of retainers and hangers-on from one luxury hotel to another in the four corners of the world.

When Hughes died of heart failure in 1976 and was flown to a Texan hospital, medics were unable to identify him. He had not been seen publicly or photographed in 20 years. His fingerprints were lifted and sent to the FBI to prove who he was. X-rays taken at his autopsy revealed fragments of hypodermic needles broken off in his arms.

Henry Ford[4] was arguably the most influential figure in the history of manufacturing, Apart from making cars, Ford spent most of his life making headlines, not all of them flattering. By any measure Ford was a one-off. It seems remarkable, for example, that someone who practically invented the 20th-century motor industry was brought up on a farm run entirely on horse-power. When he left his father's homestead in 1879 to find his fortune in Detroit, three-quarters of Americans still lived on the land. He walked to the city to look for work in its machine shops.

His radical approach to making motor cars earned him many enemies. When he announced that he would pay his workers $5 a day – more than double the prevailing rate – he was attacked by other car producers as a 'mad socialist'. Yet his flawed genius triumphed: the Ford Motor Company quickly gained world leadership in mass-produced vehicles. Key to his astounding success was introducing new production methods that cut the time needed to produce a chassis from 728 minutes to a staggering 93 minutes. In pursuit of his dream of corporate self-sufficiency Ford bought up every element needed to protect and control his production process: railroads, coal mines, timberland and sawmills, iron ore mines and ore freighters, even a glassworks.

But away from the business, the real Henry Ford was beset by many demons. In 1915 he chartered an ocean liner to carry himself and a party of pacifists to Europe; they hoped to end the war through a process of 'continuous mediation'. In 1918 he bought a newspaper, *The Dearborn Independent*, and used it to publish a series of attacks on 'The International Jew', a mythical character Ford blamed for financing war. In 1927 he retracted his comments and sold the paper. Instead, he turned to organising old-fashioned dances and invited capitalists, European royalty and company executives to have a go at the polka, the Roger de Coverley, the mazurka, the

Virginia reel and the quadrille. He experimented with soybeans for food and durable goods and sponsored a weekly radio hour on which quaint essays were read to 'plain folks'.

But one obsession was never really beaten. When Hitler's National Socialists began to take a grip on Germany's soul, Henry Ford stepped forward to help the Fuhrer. Ford gave the Nazis thousands of dollars to reprint anti-Jewish pamphlets in German translations. Further thousands were passed over to Hitler via a grandson of the ex-Kaiser. In July 1938, on Ford's seventy-fifth birthday, Hitler awarded him the Grand Cross of the Supreme Order of the German Eagle – the highest decoration that could be given to a non-German citizen. Ford was the first American and only the fourth person in the world to receive this medal. Among this elite band was Benito Mussolini.

It is hardly surprising that many corporate emperors turn loopy. The obsession they have applied to making their company great becomes, in time, a clinical obsession. The compulsive mentality that makes the corporation succeed becomes an obsessive-compulsive disorder, expressed through things like Hughes' terror of germs. The emperor turns paranoid, because a very controlling person has become out of control. He wants to control and therefore the feeling develops that he can never control – the desire can only be satisfied if he controls everything, which is obviously impossible. Nearly all highly successful people have obsessive tendencies, because they have succeeded by focusing on a very narrow route. This narrow focus invariably means it cannot be integrated into that individual's normal life – and this turns into clinical compulsion.

Despite such distractions, many of these companies became sprawling international business empires feeding on the unprecedented economic expansion of the long boom that began after the Second World War. In doing so, those companies shifted from a human-scale psyche – that of their founders – to a technocratic corporate mentality embedded in layer upon layer of management, a mentality based almost entirely on the notion of mistrust. The origins of this mistrust mentality are to be found in the pioneering work of a Scottish railway engineer, David McCallum, who developed the first organisation charts for the New York & Erie Railroad in the 1850s as a means of apportioning blame in the event of a rail accident. Over time the same multi-layered pyramid structure became the operational norm for most business corporations.

This shift to a blame-centred, multi-tiered bureaucracy designed for the supervision of the 'unreliable' lower ranks had enormous implications for the evolution of the corporate psyche. Often it made organisations risk-averse and opposed to change, or blinkered to important future trends. It left them prone to misreading the market, misunderstanding what their customers wanted and/or ignoring their wider social responsibilities, and suffering potentially lethal damage to their reputation as a result. Such weaknesses still afflict even the biggest and most successful companies, as we have seen with IBM and its failure to grasp the early opportunity of the PC and the operating systems that went with it. IBM survived and re-invented itself, but many other companies did not make it and joined the ranks of disappeared corporate names that once proudly populated the league tables of Forbes and Fortune.

Those examples apart, many senior corporations did survive the transition from one-man show to hierarchical pyramid and hitched a ride on the mass consumer revolution of the post-war years. These companies have grown to colossal size with profits to match. No doubt their century-long transformation into global enterprises was assisted by periods of clear managerial thinking founded on a sound psychological state. But for much of that time they were the walking wounded; few corporations can claim to have a psychological heritage unblemished by dysfunctional intervals. As with people, no organisation is perfect.

Indeed, it is intriguing to note how often magic, superstition, the dark arts and other unlikely elements have, in different ways, found their way into the corporate cocktail. If nothing else, this is evidence that people regard the corporation as a being, 'an entity unto itself' capable of witchcraft and wizardry. Take the story of Procter & Gamble, for many commentators the gold standard name in fast-moving consumer goods. It is also one of a small band of corporate giants that trace their roots back to before 1900. Founded by two immigrants to the United States from England and Ireland, P&G produced its first soap bars and candles in 1837 and never ventured further than Cincinnati until 1904. Like other 19th-century start-ups, real growth came after the Second World War; not until 1948 did the company deem its international operations sizeable enough to create an Overseas Division. Despite its slow start, P&G today has annual revenues of over $50 billion and Hall of Fame status as one of the small band of corporations that have made it onto the Fortune 500 list every year since it was launched in 1955.

But though one cannot challenge its undoubted successes, the company has been dogged by bizarre allegations of links to the Devil. It received unwanted media publicity in the 1980s when an unfounded rumour spread that the logo P&G had used for many years was in fact a satanic symbol. The accusation was based on a passage in the Bible, specifically Revelation 12:1, which states: 'And there appeared a great wonder in heaven; a woman clothed with the sun, and the moon under her feet, and upon her head a crown of twelve stars.' Since P&G's logo consisted of a man's face on a moon surrounded by 13 stars, some denounced it as a satanic mockery of the heavenly symbol alluded to in that Biblical verse. Others pointed out that when reflected in a mirror one could make out in the moon's face the numbers 666. On this, Revelation 13:18 says: 'If anyone has insight, let him calculate the number of the beast, for it is a man's number. His number is 666.'

P&G was deluged by thousands of phone calls about its alleged links to the forces of darkness – 15,000 a month at one point. Many were inspired by fliers claiming that 10 per cent of P&G profits went to the Church of Satan. The logo was changed to its current design, a simple rendition in blue of the letters P and G. But the accusations of satanic connections persisted. In the 1990s the issue resurfaced; stories circulated that the company's president had admitted P&G's diabolical links on a prominent TV show. The company has sued numerous times to defend its good name, but no doubt the weird – if baseless – allegations will surface yet again.

Even stranger is the constant and totally unwarranted targeting of Virgin Group founder-boss Richard Branson for his alleged devilish credentials. Branson – voted one of the 100 Top Britons in a recent poll – is widely condemned as satanic or an unbeliever by elements of the new online counter-culture spawned by the Internet. He features, for example, on the Celebrity Atheist List alongside Woody Allen, Bob Geldof, Angelina Jolie and the late Marlon Brando. He figures regularly on websites and blogs about the Antichrist. One contributor notes tersely: 'The last time I flew Virgin there were three sixes in the flight number.' And then there is liquidfreak.com, which asks quite simply: 'Why is Richard Branson actually the Devil? Should one man with so much influence and power be trusted?' Bloggers now see him as a routine focus for their online vitriol. It seems deeply ironic that Branson was himself a counter-culture entrepreneur when he first started out on the road to tycoon alley.

Case Study: Virgin' on the Psychotic?

Richard Branson's first serious foray into business was a mail-order record venture he launched in 1969, at the age of 19. But from the earliest years he had entrepreneur running through his blood. As a youngster he earned extra cash growing Christmas trees. In the mid-'60s, while still at school, he spent every waking hour trying to establish a counter-culture magazine called *Student*. He used the school's pay-phone to sell advertising space and cajoled literary luminaries such as Jean-Paul Sartre and James Baldwin to contribute. One interview quotes him as saying: 'Selling advertising is a gruesome job and very good grounding for becoming an entrepreneur. I learned a bit of bullshit early on.' There was also his Students Advisory Centre – set up principally to help pregnant girls find a sympathetic doctor who would perform an abortion.

In 1970 Branson was prosecuted for using the word 'venereal' in a leaflet for the Centre. He lost the case and was fined £7 – about $10. These origins of the Branson business empire nevertheless offer a fascinating opening chapter to the story of a now-global corporation that spans airlines, holidays, wine, retailing, cosmetics, even bridal wear. But those same roots also flag up a theme that weaves like a blood-red thread through Branson's business progress. That theme is sex. History records his overcrowded late-'60s offices as being 'packed with sexy young girls'. Down the years there are endless pictures of PR events dripping with scantily clad tabloid models, with Branson in the thick of it. There are promotional occasions where Richard has seized an unsuspecting female and twirled her upside down. There's the episode where he wagers friends on a skiing trip that he will streak, naked, down the piste for a £10 bet. Nobody takes him on, but he does it anyway.

Even the passing years have failed to cool the Branson ardour. During a business trip to Australia in 2002, Branson launched his Virgin Blue airline with publicity bashes featuring him up close and personal with busty brunettes. One Australian newspaper marked the occasion by coining a new unit of measurement. It is somewhere between a millimetre and a micron. It is called 'a branson': 'the regular distance between Sir Richard Branson and a supermodel'. Knowing all this, it is hardly surprising Richard Branson called his company Virgin. Or that his corporate colour is the bright red that psychologists associate with sex and passion.

Branson has kept tight, hands-on control of his company as it has ballooned in size and global reach. By the beginning of the 21st century Virgin comprised some 200 businesses employing over 25,000 people with annual revenues exceeding $6 billion. Branson's personal wealth has been estimated at around $1.7 billion. It is a truly world brand. Not bad for a near-sighted dyslexic called Richard.

But accurate knowledge about the Virgin Group is a rare commodity. Many of Branson's commercial activities have offshore status and what can be gleaned gives a very patchy picture. An attempt by *The Economist* to trawl through the offshore maze concluded that many Virgin companies made little or no money. Some ventures, such as vodka, cola and clothing have struggled or gone under. Maybe this helps explain Richard Branson's legendary 'thriftiness'. Despite his billionaire wealth, Richard the Lionhearted is renowned for rarely picking up a restaurant bill. He readily admits he never carries cash and bums money off his friends. Uncharitable observers note that even his 'luxuries' have to pay their way: his family holiday home on Necker Island in the Caribbean is available for rent to any well-heeled beachcomber.

Virgin clearly falls into our category of 'founder-leader' companies and one needs to ask whether this poses serious questions about the future of the business. Everything indicates that Branson is still an adolescent. He dresses like a teenager; he's a chronic prankster. He wears women's clothes to shock people. He once arranged to have a friend's house burgled for a joke. He loves to surround himself with sexy-looking girls.

For a guy in his fifties this begins to take on a worrying dimension. He seems stuck in the adolescent phase of his life and the danger is that the Virgin business will itself become stuck there as well. An adolescent says: 'I'll try anything – because I can.' Branson seems to be following the same route, exemplified by the profusion of ventures he starts up. He wants to do everything – bridal wear, contraceptives, books, finance, planes … He recently started up a bespoke tailoring business for men who pick up their new suits at their flight destination. Now there's talk of him going into oil refining. Where will it all end?

The central business issue here is: What is the image of Virgin – and does this image comply with Branson's self-view? It seems clear that public perceptions about the Virgin empire will increasingly clash with what Branson says it is. He often says he is the underdog, fighting for the little guy. We saw that in his 'dirty tricks' legal battle with British Airways. The general public know Virgin is anything but a little guy – it is a multi-billion-dollar global colossus. For a time a gap between the two – a degree of bullshit – can be maintained. But this is not open-ended. Richard Branson needs to re-define what he is now, not what he was in the 1960s, and come to terms with this in a business context.

The $8 billion-a-year Heinz food empire, meanwhile, was founded on a quite different belief in the power of numbers and an amateur, but highly effective, assessment of the consumer psyche. The son of working-class German immigrants living in western Pennsylvania in the 1850s, Henry Heinz was growing his own vegetables when still in short pants. By the time he was 12 he had a horse-drawn cart, a growing list of customers and access to his mother's recipes for condiments such as horseradish. Even at such a tender age his business approach reflected a shrewd understanding of consumer sensitivities, above all their desire for honesty. Other producers invariably sold horseradish in dark green jars to disguise the fact they had bulked out their product by adulterating it with fillers such as leaves, turnip and wood fibre. To give his horseradish a distinctive appeal he bottled it in clear glass and gave out samples. Customers liked what they saw. Food, after all, is ingested and people are infinitely fussy about what they put in their mouth. It was an early, and effective, example of the power of truth and clear thinking in achieving business success.

Heinz later wrote about how he deliberately set out to focus on customers' suspicion of food they could not see and offer products that 'set purity and quality above everything else in their preparation'. But he also borrowed from the realms of superstition and the unknown when he chose '57 Varieties' as the sub-text to his Heinz brand. Henry had an instinctive understanding of the mystical power of numbers and was prompted to deploy them to boost his business prospects after seeing a shoe store advertising '21 styles' when riding an elevated train in New York. He later commented: 'I counted up how many products we had and I went well beyond 57, but 57 kept coming up in my mind. Seven, seven – there are so many illustrations of the psychological influence of that figure … "58 Varieties" or "59 Varieties" just didn't appeal.'

His fixation with the number seven strongly suggests that Heinz was a keen reader of the very same Book of Revelation. The Book is stuffed with references to this digit: the seven churches in the province of Asia, seven golden lamp-stands, seven stars, seven spirits, seven seals, seven angels, seven trumpets, seven plagues, seven heads, seven hills, seven kings, seven bowls ... But then, if seven shifts products, who can possibly complain?

Surprisingly, given this penchant for numbers, Henry Heinz' infant business went bust in 1875 when an excess of confidence led it to get its sums wrong and overspend on processing a bumper crop of cucumbers. But Henry subsequently rallied and re-launched the business with a new speciality – tomato ketchup. Here again we see some very rudimentary psychology put to work: to satisfy well-researched customer expectations of a suitably viscous red flow, Heinz ketchup was designed to pour at a maximum speed of 0.28 miles per hour. The rest, as they say, is food history.

Other old-timers have not fared so well. Levi Strauss, for instance, was established in the mid-19th century, but the company would encounter severe commercial turbulence in the late 1990s and beyond when fashion tastes changed and Levi Strauss as an organisation did not. The lessons of their troubles are examined later. But the recent difficulties at Levi Strauss echo the travails that overtook British clothing and furniture retailer Laura Ashley, which, though boasting a less-impressive heritage, nevertheless fell victim to resting far too long on its laurels, as well as on its increasingly outdated floral prints.

Case Study: Riches to Rags

As Oscar Wilde might have put it, for a company to lose one chief executive is a misfortune. To lose two in as many months is downright careless.

The rise and fall of Laura Ashley is punctuated with such mini-disasters; two CEOs resigned in November 2004 and January 2005. But the broad sweep of the fashion and furnishing retailer's 50-year history is more akin to a cautionary nursery tale than an adult business narrative. You know, the one about the wolf in floral clothing lying in wait in the forest for little-girl-lost. Not only has the company had more comebacks than the average bungee jump, but many constantly ask why the business still bothers to exist at all.

One clue to the core problems that have long beset Laura Ashley can be found in a BBC report on the company in 1999, after yet another sign of revival in its switchback fortunes. 'The business', runs the storyline, 'is based in Wales and run by a mix of Americans, a Filipino and Malaysians, yet Laura Ashley has always been the epitome of Englishness.' How did the company find itself in this peculiar state?

The business traces its roots back to the 1950s when Laura, then pregnant, started silk-screening her designs onto scarves and napkins at the marital home in London's Pimlico district. Her husband Bernard soon decided to quit his City job and join her in setting up a workshop in Sussex.

The years pass and, despite the odd mishap, the business flourishes. By the 1980s the company and its 500 outlets around the world seem set for a prosperous future. But in 1985 tragedy struck when Laura died on her 60th birthday after falling down a flight of stairs. Nevertheless, in 1986 Bernard Ashley decided to float the family venture. The £270 million stock market flotation was heavily over-subscribed.

But things were moving on in the fashion and furnishings game. Consumer tastes were turning away from the country cottage ethos of the early Laura Ashley years towards sharper, more modern ideas from younger designers. The signature floral designs that had given Laura Ashley its pre-eminence were rapidly losing their bloom. In an effort to revive the business a succession of outside managers were brought in. Even so, analysts backed the company's future. In 1994 an article in the respected *Harvard Business Review* – *'Laura Ashley: Rebuilding and Transforming a Global Brand'* [5] – even suggested that the silver bullet of successful corporate re-invention had at last been found. But it was a false dawn.

In 1995 the company decided to tap into what it perceived to be the enormous unexploited potential of the US market. The blueprint was to invest heavily in large stores, mostly located in out-of-town shopping malls – a fundamental break with the small, homely shops US customers had known for years. This US expansion programme failed. In 1999 Laura Ashley announced it was selling all its shops in North America for a dollar, after the company's bankers told it that financial support for the enterprise would stop if its US outlets stayed part of the group. The finger of failure was pointed at the poor performance of its 32 largest stores – the cornerstone of that mid-'90s survival plan. Meanwhile, senior managers came and went. In the words of one commentator at the time: 'The departure of Laura Ashley chief executives has become an almost regular event now, with eight in all attempting to help recapture past glory.'[6]

In 2004 yet another attempt to revamp the company's clothing range failed. Fashion sales crashed by more than a third as shoppers rejected the chain's attempt to attract younger customers. Even worse, a company that owed its original success to its essential 'Englishness' – a creative observation, not a chauvinistic one – had been steadily overtaken by a shareholding and management structure that was anything but. Majority ownership passed to Malaysia's Malayan United Industrie. One financial analyst has summed up the plight of Laura Ashley in blunt terms. 'It is a bit of a shrivelled husk of a company … It is all pretty odd with its Malaysian owners seemingly just shuffling the deckchairs [on the Titanic].' The company's shares, which peaked in the mid-'90s at more than £2, had dropped to around 10 pence ten years later.

It seems to us that this is a classic example of a company failing to adjust to major changes in the nature of the external competitive environment. The reasons for this failure to adapt lay deep in the subconscious of the company, which stayed rooted in its originating heritage of a 1950s 'cottage industry' business. While fashion and design tastes changed over the decades, Laura Ashley stuck with its founding formula.

But then, great age is not necessarily a guarantee of corporate wisdom. Coca-Cola was invented by an Atlanta pharmacist in 1886 as a headache tonic – in its first year total sales reached just $50. Like most other phase-one corporations, Coke's growth accelerated strongly with the globalisation of markets that began in the late 1940s. Today it owns the world's most recognised trade mark, sells over $20 billion worth of beverages a year and has regularly featured in the Fortune list of the world's most admired companies. But Coke has endured dicey moments when flawed strategic thinking lured it into dangerous experiments with its core brand. In May 1985, after a $4 million research project, Coca-Cola brought out a new Coke formula with the intention of retiring the old version. To everyone's surprise, the intense loyalty of American consumers towards old Coke were such that the product had to be kept on the market under the name Coke Classic. Here, too, there is strong evidence of a complacent or arrogant psyche dictating a course of action that was out of step with market realities.

Coca-Cola today is still almost exclusively in the beverage business. But other senior corporations have stayed successful by constantly re-inventing themselves in keeping with a clear-headed appraisal of future market opportunities. Thomas Edison started what became General Electric in a barn in 1892 to take advantage of new markets based around electricity. For decades the company ploughed the same predictable furrow – light bulbs, electric fans, heaters and cookers. But the company changed beyond recognition in the post-war era from a maker of electrical products into a diversified financial empire with huge media interests. This transformation owes much to the vision of Ralph Cordiner, who became CEO in 1953 and took a hard look at how the company operated before setting new directions. Today's GE is in reality a young company, re-invented for the entertainment and financial services sectors under the remorseless and steely guidance of Jack Welch. It is probably the most successful corporation ever and offers powerful lessons in how to make the transition from a one-man corporate persona to a complex, but psychologically well-tuned, global eminence.

Britain has also had its corporate pioneers and they, too, had to make the transition from early years indelibly stamped with the persona of their founding fathers, many of whom were Quakers or followers of some other non-conformist Protestant persuasion, to the post-war age of fast-growing juggernauts driven by Peter Drucker's professional managers with their bureaucratic mentality. Visitors to the London headquarters of Shell or Unilever in the 1960s, for instance, could have been forgiven for thinking themselves in some soulless civil service department. There were numbers or formal names on the office doors and one could discern the managerial status of the occupants by the size of desk, the quality of curtains or carpet, the number of managers per room and – the most telling status symbol of all – whether they had a key to the executive lavatory.

Understanding the inner personality traits of these big, bureaucratic, first-phase corporations had, of course, become a minority sport after Lillian Gilbreth and other early proponents of organisation behaviour had taken a back seat. But an amusing yet also very perceptive study of Anglo-Saxon corporations, published in 1972, offers an original insight. In *The Company Savage*,[7] Cambridge-trained anthropologist Martin Page identifies remarkably close similarities between practices in old-style trans-Atlantic companies and the functioning of African tribes. The central theme of the book is that tribes and corporations have the same attachment to the notion of 'spirit' and that this spirit is specific to each organisation: 'A tribe's or corporation's spirit usually possesses a distinct personality. It can be relentlessly cheerful and derring-do or one with a sense of mission to uplift the tone of the civilisation that uses its products. It can be stodgily conservative and withdrawn into itself or brashly extrovert, or relaxed and over-complacent, or tetchily neurotic – anything, in fact, a person can be.'

Whatever their spiritual differences, these first-phase enterprises were soon to be joined by a new post-war strain of the corporate gene that was to transform the business scene as well as our way of life. The biggest product brand on Earth, McDonalds, was born in 1955. But most of the rest were ventures created by children of the Sixties or later. Nike, Microsoft, Apple, Body Shop, Ben & Jerry's, Virgin, Intel, Cisco, Dell

– they represent a breed of companies that revolutionised the style and flavour of everyday living and stood apart from the clunky, smokestack mentality of the Henry Ford industrial model. With their dress-down ideologies and apparent rejection of old-style corporate habits, these companies have influenced every aspect of our lives with innovative and adventurous products and services. None of these names existed in 1960; most of them weren't even around in 1970. They have invariably created an entirely new business sector or challenged and redesigned how things are done in mature ones. They have taken on powerful, established enterprises with equally powerful global brands – and beaten them.

In the process they have also rapidly carved out a sizeable chunk of the global business pie. The world's biggest corporation and now also the number-one private employer on the planet – Wal-Mart – achieved that status in just four decades. More importantly, this new breed – and, later, the dot.com ventures that would proliferate after the creation of the World Wide Web in the 1990s – brought to the marketplace a psyche that was unburdened by long heritage and deeply embedded behavioural habits developed over generations. They began their lives with a clean psychological slate. Some, like Ben & Jerry's, were bought out by the old order – in their case by Unilever, leaving behind some curious footnotes on entrepreneurial eccentricity. But in most cases they are still run by the same self-starter entrepreneurs who created them; they represent a special category of 'founder-leader' organisations that have inner personalities that inevitably reflect the psychological characteristics of their creators. It will be both fascinating and instructive, when the time arrives, to see how these companies manage the transition to a post-founder-leader corporate afterlife.

Case Study: Flower-Power Ice Cream Goes Bananas

True sons of the flower-power 1960s were Ben Cohen and Jerry Greenfield. They met in a 7th-grade gym class in 1963 and were henceforth inseparable. With the help of a $5 correspondence course they mastered the art of making ice cream. In 1978 they opened for business as Ben & Jerry's in a renovated gas station in Vermont.

From the start B&J's was the ultimate New Age enterprise. They held free summer movie festivals, projecting films onto the outside walls of their Vermont plant. And they cooked up a never-ending stream of whacky ice cream recipes: Makin' Whoopie Pie, Honey I'm Home, Karamel Sutra, The Full VerMonty. Their fluffy company mission statement says: 'We seek and support non-violent ways to achieve peace and justice.' Make ice cream, not war.

By 1984 the company was selling $4 million worth of ice cream a year, with annual sales growth topping 100 per cent. They proved their small entrepreneur, community-loving credentials by creating the Ben & Jerry Foundation in 1985 to fund local projects. In 1988 those credentials were endorsed by President Reagan, who named them US Small Business Persons of The Year. Then, in April 2000, their small business ethos deserted them. They sold their company to food giant Unilever for $326 million.

Sometimes it is instructive to take a closer look at the psychological make-up of people like Ben Cohen. One celebrated episode resulted in a boycott of B&J ice cream parlours by US police trade unions after Ben decided to use his website comment column to announce his support for the Free Mumia Jamal Movement. Jamal had been convicted of murdering a police officer in Philadelphia. It was a particularly horrendous killing. Witnesses testified they saw Jamal shoot the officer in the back then empty the gun into the victim's face. Ben Cohen wrote that he felt Jamal had not been given a fair trial. Critics replied that the case was widely referred to in the press as 'a prosecutor's dream', it was such an open-and-shut affair. Jamal had been arrested at the scene within minutes, still holding the gun, and a legion of witnesses queued up to give testimony against him.

But surely the booby prize for Nice Guy of The Year must go to Ben for his ill-timed website criticism of US defence spending. On 4 September 2001 – just seven days before the attacks on the World Trade Center and the Pentagon – Ben posted a spoof job offer for millions to read: 'ENEMY WANTED: serious enemy wanted to justify Pentagon budget increase. Defense contractors desperate. Interested enemies send letter and photo or video (threatening, OK) to Enemy Search Committee...'

Perhaps all that money from Unilever had gone to his head.

This is a fascinating phenomenon – the successful entrepreneur who mutates into an oddball activist for causes that have nothing to do with his core product, in this case ice cream. The story is reminiscent of the bizarre tale of David Koresh, leader of the Branch Davidian cult, who died in a siege inferno fighting the FBI in Waco, Texas in 1993. Ben Cohen thinks his behaviour is very 'New Age' – he's anti anything that is accepted. This kind of personality will use any aspect of spirituality to put across its viewpoint. They appear to be more 'honest' than they actually are. Now this image may last for a while, but not for ever. The lesson here is that whatever is 'alternative' as a business idea raises genuine issues about sincerity. And eventually that impacts on the business.

Luckily for Ben Cohen, he's already cashed in his chocolate chips by selling out to precisely the kind of corporate giant he seemed to despise. But perhaps one is also entitled to question just how 'socially aware' was his conscience, as opposed to his merely having an understandable desire to become rich. After all, his products brought yet more sugar into the diet of a nation of 'fatties' beset by a pandemic of obesity and associated diseases such as diabetes and heart problems that is driving up the country's healthcare costs by countless billions, with worse predicted in years to come. The last thing Americans – and citizens of other countries in the rich world – need is another excuse to eat ice cream, with or without the flower-power flourish.

While ice cream took off many Internet ventures, of course, perished in the dot.com bust of 2000/01. But some have survived and become global players. Companies like Yahoo!, eBay and Google – which operate in online virtual space – bring a new dimension to the corporate universe.

Even though they have no physical presence manifested through tangible products or high-street shop fronts, they are corporations none the less – each of them now valued in excess of $45 billion – and rank alongside Nike and the others as companies shaped by the people who set them up. Here, too, we will discover over the next few years just how many of these virtual enterprises will survive the transition to new management and what psychological traumas they may suffer in making that shift.

Corporate Biology

But we should take great care to distinguish between the Anglo-Saxon corporate model – both old and new – and those of their cousins in continental Europe and Asia. Although a long-standing theory has stressed the role of the Protestant work ethic in planting the seeds of capitalism in northern Europe, this approach is too simplistic. Across mainland Europe business traditions differ from those in the English-speaking world and even from one country to another. These differences have important implications for how their companies are perceived, how they function and how their personas evolve over time.

As Hampden-Turner and Trompenaars have observed about the world's third-largest economy: 'German-style capitalism is not simply closer geographically to the ex-communist world, it is also closer psychologically and ideologically.'[8] Germany was a late industrialiser that endeavoured to foster popular consent through social benefits and inclusive labour policies. As a nation it had suffered continual political and economic trauma – hyperinflation, military defeat, occupation, territorial division – that ingrained an instinct of caution and a belief in industrial method. Most of its corporations are in the manufacturing and engineering sectors, where science rather than imagination rules.

Compared to the laissez-faire economic principles of the Anglo-Saxon world, Germans have preferred managed competition and protection. But they have also adopted a philosophical stance that regards the corporate whole as more important than its constituent parts. Despite their preference for engineering-based enterprises, they tend to see corporations not as machine-like entities but as a group of related persons working together. Interlocking boards with overlapping directors and long-term links with particular German banks gave them a kind of Masonic hue. The practice of *Mitbestimmung* – worker co-determination – required of any German company with more than 2000 employees, puts workers and shareholders on supervisory boards and promotes a communitarian outlook and sense of common purpose. One is reminded of the Borg – the monolithic community in TV's Star Trek. Unlike the self-interested Anglo-Saxon enterprise, the German corporation is a social association first, profit-earner second.

The characteristics of French corporations reflect that country's traditional attachment to philosophical and intellectual process and its *étatiste* culture. The enterprise has been seen as an entity greater than the people who work for it, but one that is subservient to broader French society. Henri Fayol, a French mine manager born in 1841 and accredited as being the first to formulate the principles of management, summed up this distinctive view: 'in a business the interest of one employee or group of employees should not prevail over that of the concern … and the interest of the State should have pride of place'. This line of thinking prompted the one-time boss of car-maker Peugeot, Jacques Calvet, to stand on its head the maxim beloved of US businessmen and politicians: 'What's good for General Motors is good for America.' As Calvet put it: 'I consider what is good for France is good for Peugeot.'

Fayol spoke of the organisation as a *corps social*, literally a body corporate – a biological entity. The French predilection for rule by elites (fittingly a French word) educated in the country's prestigious *grandes écoles* ensured a corporate style totally different from Anglo-Saxon business organisations. Instead of a careerist, pecuniary management environment driven by the search for personal advancement and marked by frequent job changes, the French corporation developed as a family-like, cohesive community directed from within and jealous of its tribe-like values. Even today, 80 per cent of French companies employ graphologists to analyse the handwritten letters asked of all job applicants, so as to gain an insight into their social and psychological suitability. Lifetime employment was long the norm; promotion was from within. Failed or underperforming managers were not sacked, but instead were 'parked' elsewhere within the organisation where they could do no harm – a phenomenon also observed in Japanese corporate life.

It is not surprising, given these observations, that many large continental European companies have remained family-run concerns for years after their founding generation had passed on, a factor that has fostered a climate of corporate insularity and distrust of alien business cultures. When tyre manufacturer Michelin – which now rivals Goodyear as the world's biggest – was founded by André and Edouard Michelin in 1889 it was created not as 'Inc.' or 'Ltd', as were US and British corporations, but as a legal entity known as a Partnership by Shares, with successive generations of the family involved in senior management. At the time of writing, one of the company's three Managing Partners is named Edouard Michelin.

A recent survey of the world's 250 biggest family-owned companies by US-based *Family Business* magazine confirmed this continental preference for family-controlled corporations, many of them hidden behind complex shareholding arrangements and trusts. Although it shows the United States to have a great many family-run enterprises, this is not surprising in an economy over ten times bigger than that of any European country. The important fact, however, is that practically every US corporate giant is owned by its stockholders and run by professional managers. In contrast, the list revealed France to have 17 immense business dynasties, the cream of its corporate fraternity, where a single family still holds sway; Germany had 16. The UK, in contrast, had only three. And one of those, supermarket chain Sainsbury's, hardly qualifies, as the Sainsbury family has just 38 per cent of the company's shares and plays little or no role in management. It is perhaps no surprise that Spain, which has eight family concerns on the $billion-plus revenue list and still carries the imprint of the corporatist years of the Franco regime, has a Chair for Family-Owned Companies at one of its leading universities.

Legal constructs like that adopted by Michelin had the added benefit of making unwanted takeovers more difficult, a consideration that plays big among France's fiercely nationalistic – and anti-Anglo-Saxon – business community. When, in the summer of 2005, Pepsi Cola mounted a hostile bid for food giant Danone – the world's number one in bottled water and run by the Riboud family – it was as if the nation faced military invasion. President Chirac took a public stand against this dastardly threat to French corporate pride. Prime Minister Dominique de Villepin went even further: 'Danone is obviously one of our industrial treasures and we will of course defend the interests of France.' In keeping with this corporate chauvinism the French government announced in September 2005 a list of ten business sectors that would enjoy state protection against foreign takeover.

This family tradition has important implications for the psychological evolution of continental European companies. For different reasons, the concept of family also impacts Anglo-Saxon companies that have moved on to become incorporated bureaucracies. As Harry Levinson points out,[9] businesses have usually begun as family affairs. When they grow into huge enterprises there remains a strong urge among senior management to paint the company as 'one big family'. Sometimes a paternalistic leadership has worked hard to foster a 'family' relationship that would maximize the dependency – and hence loyalty – of its employees. But this is not without enormous risks. After all, families can be quagmires of dysfunctional relationships, with complex dynamics that can be immensely destructive. Whether the company is owned by family members or shareholders, if the dominant executive is viewed as a benevolent patriarchal figure it can have serious psychological implications for those successors who have to take over the helm in the shadow of the great man. They are now operating not as a father figure but in a fraternal role within a 'family' of peers and it is very difficult for fraternal chief executives to take what they perceive to be hostile actions against their organisational siblings. Firing a manager has overtones of fratricide. Invariably, senior management in such circumstances live in geographical proximity to one another, are members of the same golf club and socialise together at weekends. The result is an organisation frozen by inhibitions and stalked by guilt. Not the ideal way to promote a change-oriented, risk-taking corporate mindset.

Exhibit: Keep it in the Family
Europe's Corporate Dynasties

France

- Carrefour, Europe's biggest retailer, is controlled by some 60 members of the Deforrey family.

- Retail giant Auchan is 84 per cent owned by 350 members of the highly secretive Mulliez family. Employees own the rest.

- Retail-to-luxury goods company Pinault-Printemps-Redoute, with exclusive labels like Gucci and Yves St Laurent in its portfolio, is 57 per cent owned by Artémis, the investment arm of the Pinault family.

- The Peugeot family controls 42 per cent of the company's voting stock.

- Other French dynastic corporations include L'Oréal, Lagardère, Bouygues and luxury goods producer LMVH.

Germany

- The Aldi retail empire is still owned by its co-founders Theo and Karl Albrecht.

- At the time of publication, BMW, founded in 1917, was still 47 per cent owned by the reclusive widowed family heiress Johanna Quandt.

- Car parts colossus Robert Bosch, which first opened for business in 1886, remains the private property of the Bosch Foundation (with 92 per cent of its shares) and the Bosch family.

- Also among the top 250 are Tengelmann, Bertelsmann, Karstadt Quelle and the Otto Group.

Spain

- Retail-to-financial services group El Corte Inglés, the country's largest family firm, is owned by the Álvarez dynasty.

- $32-billion-turnover Banco Santander has been run by the Botín family since 1857.

- Other big family companies on the top 250 list include Banco Popular, Grupo Ferrovial, Acciona, Inditex and Mercadona.

Italy

- Century-old car makers Fiat has remained the preserve of the Agnelli family, which owns a third of the stock, with third-generation managers in charge.

- Parmalat, the vast dairy empire that collapsed at the end of 2003 after a €10 billion black hole was discovered in its accounts, was founded by the Tanzi family.

- Other seriously big Italian family enterprises are Ifi, the Agnelli holding company, Italmobiliare, ERG (which turns over $5 billion a year in oil), Benetton, Barilla and Prada.

Source: *Family Business* magazine

Eastern Spirit

At first sight there are some similarities with the continental European tradition when we look at the rise of the corporation in East Asia. But the impression is misleading. There are notable differences in the history, anthropology and psychological dimensions of how business is done in that part of the world. These differences are important factors in understanding the erratic fortunes of both Japanese and Korean companies in recent years, as they have struggled to adjust to the impact of globalisation and the rise of fast-moving and unpredictable trans-national consumer markets. Meanwhile, the rapid rise of China's economy along with a phalanx of gigantic state-owned enterprises now brings a new dimension to the challenge of the corporate game.

In the particular case of Japan the vital issue today is whether the psychological ramifications of its unique culture and language, which served it so well during its post-war recovery boom, now put the country at a serious disadvantage when confronting the demands of the 21st century. A company's corporate psyche is not only about driving appropriate behaviours that can achieve success today, but also about offering a platform for meeting the demands of the next business generation and beyond. And you do not have to be a 'bad guy' to wallow in corporate bullshit – even the nicest companies can be victims.

The East Asian region possesses the world's oldest surviving family companies and still carries the psychological legacy of an ancient system of commercial enterprises based around families or clans. Japan's Kongo Gumi, based in Osaka, was originally a temple builder founded in AD 578. It is still in business in the construction industry, along with some temple renovation, and is run by the fortieth generation of the Kongo family. As it happens, their forebears were from Korea, where family-owned companies still figure prominently in South Korean business. Five *chaebols*, or family-run industrial groups that have grown from humble origins, tower over the economy. The biggest are two electronics giants: Samsung, a $100-billion-revenue conglomerate built by the Lee family (originally to sell dried fish) and the $80 billion LG Group (originally Lucky Goldstar, a chemical company) founded by the Koo and Huh families. These two alone have a combined economic weight greater than Argentina or Iran.

The modern Japanese corporation is in one sense a major departure from the ancient clan system that preceded Japan's industrialisation, but it nevertheless has distinctive behavioural characteristics that place it apart from the Anglo-Saxon model. Where US and British corporations are entities geared to legal and standards-based considerations, their Asian counterparts are run through relationships and traditions of trust. Much of this has come from long-established business practices centred on family or group kinship, as with Korea's *chaebol* and its Japanese counterpart, the *zaibatsu* (literally 'financial cliques'). And while Anglo-

Saxon corporations usually were founded and are owned by private shareholders, Japan's *zaibatsu* invariably began through state funding before being sold by the government at low prices to certain Samurai families. Indeed, throughout the industrialisation of Japan there was to be a close inter-relationship between state influence and the success of particular enterprises. One of the major criticisms of Japan's response to the decade-long economic crisis that began in the early 1990s is that corporate boardrooms often did little more than appeal for a government-backed bail-out.

As a matter of historical fact, many of the global Japanese brands we all know today only emerged in their current form after defeat and occupation by the United States in 1945 and a consequent opening of the country to American business influences. They would nevertheless soon become major world players. Toyota – originally a manufacturer of weaving machinery – launched its first small car in 1947. The company would subsequently become widely acknowledged as the touchstone for manufacturing excellence. The Sony brand was not officially registered until 1955 – but it would not be long before it conquered the world with revolutionary products like the transistor radio, Walkman and later PlayStation. Toshiba, originally a mining company, was officially incorporated under this more internationally user-friendly name in 1978 and began carving out an impressive chunk of the global market for consumer electronics.

But it would be a serious mistake to group these companies with US and British multinationals. Japan's corporate landscape has been shaped by a long and quite separate heritage and psychological outlook. Many of the country's leading business names are, in reality, a *zaibatsu* in modern guise. Mitsui was founded as a family business in 1673. Mitsubishi, or 'Three Diamonds', was established as a financial administrator in a samurai-controlled region of Japan before the Meiji Revolution. It did not mutate into a car producer until 1917. Suzuki started life as a sugar importer in the 19th century. Sumitomo Corporation, which now ranks in the world's top 150 corporations, was created by Masatomo Sumitomo in 1590 as a mining and smelting concern. Today, over four centuries on, the company's website proudly proclaims: 'The "Founder's Precepts" of Masatomo Sumitomo still drive the Sumitomo Corporation's spirit.' This belief in the idea of a corporate spirit – or psyche – pervades the Japanese way of thinking about business.

Even Japanese companies of 20th-century origin follow this distinctive approach, which relies on a deeply philosophical view of company purpose. Konosuke Matsushita, who founded the mighty Matsushita Electric Company – best known today through its Panasonic and Technics brands – in 1918 with the invention of a double-outlet plug, put his finger on the difference between a US or British corporation and its Japanese competitor. Writing in 1985, he said: 'For you the essence of management is getting the idea out of the heads of the bosses into the hands of labour. For us the art of management is the art of mobilising and pulling together the intellectual resources of all the employees in the service of the firm.'[10] But does this fundamental difference in psychological culture carry any lessons for the theme of this book? Part of the answer may lie in Japan's post-war experience.

During the 1960s and '70s the rise of Japan's economy, with huge growth rates and a massive expansion of exports, began transforming the country into a major force in world business. Initially this was dismissed as the result of the country's skill for borrowing Western industrial technology and management ideas and giving them a Japanese veneer – a copycat economy tied to the apron strings of Western corporate prowess. One or two more prescient commentators saw differently. Herman Kahn, director of US-based futurology 'think tank' the Hudson Institute, wrote in his 1970 study, *The Emerging Japanese Superstate*:[11] 'The time has come to ask what this likely economic development means for Japan and the world ... I myself will be surprised if by the end of the century they do not become *dai-ichi* [number one].'

In the years thereafter Japanese corporations and their innovative products became synonymous with world-class business thinking.

Traditional trading houses became powerful international enterprises; industrial companies, ravaged by war, revived; totally new business brands conquered world markets in cars, motorcycles and electronics. Japanese banks rubbed shoulders with US and European giants in the top league. Trade surpluses soared. The country's currency became a key player in global financial markets.

With its copycat image long gone, Japan became a laboratory for the pursuit of manufacturing excellence, daring innovation and 'consensual management'. In this, students of Japan's remarkable turnaround from defeat and occupation at the end of the Second World War made constant reference to the unique characteristics of what they called the 'Japanese Mind' and its role in giving Japanese business its apparent edge. At its heart was a value system that put hierarchy and family before the individual and required its organisations – public and private – to be run by a process of 'group-centred decision-making'. The crunch question is whether that value system would be sustainable beyond the post-war phase of national recovery and corporate blossoming or whether it had in it the seeds of Japan's eventual business decline.

Most analysts have been content to highlight the obvious contrasts with Western business. Kahn, for example, devoted much space to the topic of Japan's unique psycho-cultural traditions, drawing on specialist works from *The Chrysanthemum and the Sword* by Ruth Benedict[12] and R. P. Dore's *The Japanese Personality*[13] to Inatomi Eijiro's *The Japanese Mind*.[14] The picture Kahn painted was one totally removed from the individualist entrepreneurial energies that consumed business pioneers like Heinz, Lever, Edison, Nestlé and Ford. Instead, he found references to psychological characteristics that, to a Western eye, would not seem designed to foster innovative achievement or business success. Robert Huntingdon is quoted as saying: 'The Japanese personality has weak, indistinct, permeable boundaries between the self and other; is dependent as opposed to independent, group-cooperative rather than self-reliant; conforming rather than innovative.'[15] Then there is this from

Bruno Bettelheim: 'In Japan the psychoanalyst's task was seen to consist in helping the young individual to give up his search for self-identity … accepting his place within the family in the traditional subservient position of the son toward his father.' And there is also Kahn's personal conclusion that the Japanese corporation – the *zaibatsu* – is: 'a business run as an extended democratic family but in a conforming, communal-minded culture and with an authoritarian hierarchy.'

For many commentators this inclination to see the enterprise as a kind of spiritual endeavour – a 'whole' that is more than the sum of its parts – driven by a consensual, inclusive management style helped to explain the phenomenal success of Japanese corporations between the 1960s and the 1980s. Toyota's achievement in studying US production-line methods and then transforming them into world-beating manufacturing techniques has earned it a well-deserved place in business legend. Key to this was the self-same reliance on a seamless, company-wide commitment to product improvement, with every employee encouraged to 'pull together', to use Matsushita's phrase, to achieve excellence. The *kanban* system employed in Japanese factories is an interesting manifestation of this collectivist spirit. Each component in the production cycle is labelled with details of how it fits in to the whole assembly. Every part and every individual in the process, in other words, is given equal value – in the manner of musical instruments all individually contributing to the beautiful finished sound of some grand corporate orchestra.

Eijiro, meanwhile, drills deeper into this theme of a group-minded psychological environment with his illuminating take on the barriers to individualism created by the Japanese language: 'Japanese are devoid of self-consciousness … as evidenced by the lack of clear distinction between the parts of speech in Japanese as contrasted with European languages. … A Japanese sentence is a composite whole and not an aggregate of individual words and phrases. This corresponds with the fact that in actual life a Japanese has no clear consciousness of his individual self, but recognises his own existence only in the composite life of the world.'[16]

Such an observation may have little weight among European and North American readers, whose languages are, in general, fairly effective in allowing people to convey unambiguous meaning without some complex 'composite' sub-text. But it may carry extremely important consequences for how Japanese corporations function. Language, after all, is the most important means we have of analysing situations, sharing ideas, discussing options, agreeing courses of action. In the workplace and at the level of the broader organisation, language is the currency of communication and clear communication is one of the hallmarks of successful business practices. While Japan's inherently introvert corporate community was rebuilding its shattered infrastructure during the '50s and '60s, this 'composite' ethos, with its accent on sacrificing 'self' to the greater good of the whole, was probably a crucial element in getting Japan Inc. back on its feet and underpinning its impressive surge to become the world's number-two economy. In crude terms, the nation was genetically designed to 'pull together' and did so with remarkable results.

But is Japan's genetic predisposition to support a collective, hierarchical business psyche still suited to the very different corporate landscape created by the unprecedented technology explosion and social changes of the 1980s and thereafter, which dramatically changed the rules of business? Is Japan's unique psycho-cultural experience suited to the radically different markets of the 'knowledge' economy and its splintering offshoots? Just as crucial, is the country psychologically ready to deal with the looming economic threat of a resurgent China and the cultural invasion from South Korea? To slip into the vernacular, is Eijiro's elegant exposition on the complexities of Japanese language in fact merely describing a particularly subtle recipe for delusionary bullshit that has, in Japan's case, stored up trouble for the future? The rollercoaster ride of the Japanese economy – and of former corporate stars like Sony – in recent years may indeed be weak signals that the Japanese miracle is well past its sell-by date.

Rising Sun Soon to Set?

The issue is a fascinating one: can a nation's entire corporate culture generate psychological tendencies that, at first, promote world-beating recovery and business success, but then so block its capacity for change that it loses momentum and stagnates, possibly permanently? Developments in Japan – and at Sony, its most famous corporate son – offer some instructive insights.

After 30 years of breakneck growth, in 1989–90 Japan's 'bubble economy' of high land prices and inflated share markets collapsed, triggering a vicious circle of self-reinforcing business crises. Banks were saddled with huge bad debts. As a result, lending to Japanese companies dried up. One consequence was that they started moving their operations abroad, pushing up the rate of unemployment back home. With jobless numbers rising, Japanese consumer spending took a dive, in turn pushing down retail prices and squeezing corporate margins. Interest rates on private savings plummeted to near zero. Japan had entered a deflationary spiral that fed off itself. Traditional economic thinking seemed to offer no solutions; contrary to prevailing economic theory, Japan's crisis would continue right through the 1990s. Japanese commentators refer to it as the Lost Decade.

The legacy of this near-meltdown still stalks Japan's business environment. The country's hard-earned industrial prestige took a savage blow. Long-successful companies like Hitachi and Toshiba reported losses for the first time since the Second World War. In an effort to jump-start the ailing economy, the government poured billions into market-support operations. But the tide of economic woes could not be turned. National output stagnated. Government borrowing reached 130 per cent of gross national product, the highest level of any industrial nation. At its bullish height, before the downturn, the Tokyo stock market's Nikkei index stood at 40,000 points. For years it has trailed at less than half that level. And, behind the bald numbers, millions of Japanese households suddenly confronted the end of a generation of unbounded economic optimism and good living. To add to this cauldron of challenges, Japan's population has moved since the 1950s from being the youngest among the developed nations to being easily the oldest, with all the costs, tensions and pressures of adjustment this brings.

The response of corporate Japan to this massive economic crisis is very illuminating. The country's business commentators pointed out that while US corporations had been busily divesting themselves of non-core business activities so as to sharpen their competitiveness, heirs to Japan's tradition-bound zaibatsu stuck with old habits that dictated a presence in as many business sectors as possible. A conglomerate like Hitachi maintained its product portfolio across a vast spectrum of unrelated commercial interests – mainframes and PCs, lifts, industrial robots, nuclear power plants, ceramics, washing machines, even a flirtation with property development. Was this true of the country's entire corporate community – was it locked into an unrealistic taste for giganticism built around an obsession with the 'composite whole' and an in-built preference for doing things the old way?

At first glance the story of Sony – and its co-founder Akio Morita – seems to encapsulate Japan's post-war corporate saga. It is often portrayed as a bellwether of Japan's prospects in the 21st century. Groomed to succeed to a 14-generation family business – a prominent sake brewing enterprise in Nagoya – Morita chose instead the high-risk route of launching his own start-up in the rubble of defeat. With a partner and a $500 loan he founded Tokyo Telecommunications Engineering in a corner of a bombed-out store, making a range of basic household appliances. The company was to rise from these humble beginnings to straddle the global market for entertainment electronics, with a brand name that stood head and shoulders above the rest.

But a closer look reveals that Sony was a special case – in the Japanese context a corporate experiment – that nevertheless may have within it important lessons about what might be in store for Japan's business giants in the years ahead. From the beginning Morita was an independent voice in Japanese business. He was ahead of his peers in recognising the power of brand identity in building a strong market position, at a time when struggling Japanese companies sold their products under other – mainly US – brand names. He also argued that the country's closed business culture, with its spiritual bias, was an obstacle to the long-term success of Japan Inc. 'We thought', he said, 'that if we run our company the Japanese way we cannot be successful. So that's why Sony's management concept is a mixture of Japanese and western.'

Morita took his family to the United States for a while to live and absorb American ways. Searching for a brand name that would appeal to consumers across the world he combined *sonus*, the Latin for sound, with 'sonny', an American slang term for a small boy. The result was a word that meant nothing in any language but that at the same time, Morita believed, had resonance with his intended marketplace of young, music-loving customers. In the 1950s he changed the company name from Tokyo Telecommunications Engineering to its more catchy replacement. Sony never looked back.

Under Morita the company developed the first transistor radio, the Trinitron television system and other pioneering products. Morita himself was the inspiration behind the Walkman, introduced in 1979 – surely one of the hallmark popular consumer products of the 20th century. Always on the lookout for promising trends, he spotted the huge opportunity for a music device that allowed the user to listen while doing something else. He nevertheless had to fight off significant opposition within Sony from executives who insisted there was no market for such an idea. It was the first of a new generation of on-the-move products that helped the Sony brand capture the commanding heights of the mass entertainment markets of the 1980s.

But during the 1990s, with Morita no longer running the company, Sony stumbled badly. Critics noticed a slowness to act imaginatively in key business areas. It missed out on new product sectors, seemingly in the hope that major changes in the external competitive environment would fade away. In 1999 the company announced 17,000 job losses. In 2005 another 10,000 jobs worldwide faced the axe. In the intervening five years the Sony share price lost two-thirds of its value.

Case Study: Sayonara Sony?

As the impact of Japan's Lost Decade of the 1990s took hold, Sony, for so long an icon of the country's formidable corporate achievement, went into decline. Falling prices in the consumer electronics market had put margins under persistent pressure. Earnings – and the company share price – suffered. In March 1999 Sony closed 15 of its factories and made 17,000 employees redundant, something previously unheard of in Japan's job-for-life corporate culture. Symbolically, in that same year Akio Morita, Sony's inspirational co-founder, died.

Akio Morita had suffered a stroke whilst playing tennis in 1993 – the very year Japan's recession turned into long-term stagnation. The following year he retired as chairman. How would the company handle the transition from nearly half a century of exceptional personal dynamism and a management style that blended Eastern and Western business philosophies?

Industry analysts highlight a succession of company failings during the 1990s that severely eroded Sony's once-unchallenged position in the personal audio-visual market. It did not anticipate the heavy demand for flat-screen TVs. Its response to the commoditisation of TV and DVD products was 'flat-footed'. And while the rise of personal music devices – exemplified in Morita's Walkman – had put Sony on the world map as the leading global brand in this business sector, it was knocked sideways by the launch and ensuing colossal success of Apple's iPod. As it happens, the 'father of the iPod' Tony Faddell first took his revolutionary new idea to Sony, but the company rejected it. Overall, the post-Morita Sony had simply failed to keep abreast of what customers actually wanted, above all the shift to personalised music via the Internet. As industry specialist Adam Lashinsky wrote in Fortune: 'As illegal downloads exploded in popularity in the 1990s, Sony, like the rest of the music industry, froze.' [17]

To be more precise, Sony had become frozen in a time warp of its own making. The new download market was a frontal attack on Sony's desire to protect its proprietary technologies – the company had no intention of building devices that could run MP3, the popular compression technology that enables music to be downloaded, even if the youth marketplace was adopting it in droves. Instead, Sony chose to build music devices based on its own mini-disc system, leaving the MP3 market open to players with a fraction of Sony's clout in this area, including Apple. As a result, Sony missed the boat on an entire new generation of business opportunity. In Lashinsky's words: 'Apple's introduction of its iTunes music store and downloading software in 2003 was a watershed in digital music.' [18]

In April 2003, in what the world's business press dubbed 'the Sony Shock', the company announced its biggest quarterly deficit in eight years. Plans were announced to cut 20,000 jobs over the next three years. On world stock markets, Sony shares took a beating: over $8 billion was wiped off Sony's market value as investors fled. In 2005 Sony appointed Sir Howard Stringer, a Welsh-born journalist, as chairman – the first non-Japanese to hold this post in the company's 49-year history. It also announced the company's new President would be Ryoji Chubachi, who vowed in his first public utterances that Sony's future products would be more in line with what consumers want. 'Right now', he said, 'there is a gap between what consumers expect from Sony, their image of the Sony brand and reality.' The big question – for Japan's corporate family as much as for Sony alone – is whether this reality gap is a symptom of a more permanent dysfunctional condition, a sign that a generation of almost stratospheric success blinded Japan's corporate leaders to the need to re-invent themselves for the competitive challenges of a new century.

The post-Morita Sony comes across as panicky and worried. It is sacking people and overworking its staff. Even under Morita it felt it knew better than consumers when it came to product innovations – what you could call 'market arrogance'. Most Japanese corporations are the same. For example, the introduction of the phenomenally successful and ground-breaking Walkman was strongly resisted by most of the Sony board and only went ahead because of Morita's force of personality. The company's current commercial woes stem in large part from a continuing refusal to embrace radical changes in the music market and the emergence of a music-download culture. Even if Sony's new management were to rediscover the flair of the Morita years, this 'market arrogance' could spell danger ahead.

Could the troubles at Sony manifest a broader problem – that the uniquely Japanese psychological contract that underpinned the country's astonishing rise to global prominence is no longer relevant to the conditions of 21st-century business? And that the legendary corporate virtues of the 'composite whole' pulling together in the pursuit of excellence have lost their power. After all, Sony's corporate psyche embraced what it saw as the best of both business worlds – East and West – and it has now discovered that this has not protected it from the prospect of long-term decline.

Applying a psychology perspective, Japan's economic experience can be likened to an adolescent. At its peak, it could be very aggressive and jump around a lot but never acknowledge that it could get things wrong. It had never really grown up. In the 1960s, Japanese companies were pushy and patriarchal. They fought almost anything but lacked the clarity needed to see things through to an effective conclusion. Their legendary reliance on 'corporate consensus', meanwhile, is a myth disguised by a complex outer shell. In Japan, business and social cultures merge, producing a patriarchal, respectful and deferential ethos that is based essentially on fear. In one instance, fear of discovery and possible retribution from consumers and regulatory authorities seems to have driven the conduct of Snow Brand, one of Japan's biggest food companies, when it sought – unsuccessfully – to keep the lid on a product-contamination crisis.

Case Study: Corporate Snow Job*

Japan's much-vaunted corporate tradition of sacrificing 'self' to the greater good of the whole somehow evaporated when the board of the country's leading dairy-products company found itself in trouble. In 2000, large numbers of people suffered food poisoning after consuming products made by the Snow Brand Milk Products company. More than 10,000 people were affected. Official inspections revealed appalling standards of hygiene; a valve on the production line at its Osaka factory was found to be contaminated by toxin-causing bacteria. It was also discovered that the company routinely recycled old milk returned from retailers.

The company's reaction was to go into elaborate denial mode, with enormous commercial consequences. First, the company attempted to limit the public relations damage by trying to persuade local health authorities to agree a minimal product recall. City health officials responded by ordering a full recall and published the facts about the company's cover-up efforts for all to see. The company also tried to stifle the flow of information about what exactly had gone wrong and subsequently admitted falsifying details about the scale of contamination. Under a barrage of criticism for 'corporate arrogance' eight top executives resigned.

But the resignations came too late. Sales plummeted; the company's once dominant market share was savaged. Five factories were closed, soon to be followed by three more. The company was to report losses of $430 million for the year. A new President was appointed, who announced a major drive to improve Snow Brand's record on corporate and social responsibility. But something was rotten in this particular corporate kingdom: in early 2002 the company's meat processing unit Snow Brand Food was caught mislabelling nearly 14 tons of beef products in order to claim government compensation under a 'mad cow' subsidy scheme. In February 2002, with its share price rapidly heading south, Snow Brand Food announced it would liquidate the business by the following April. In May the company's shares were delisted from the Tokyo Stock Exchange.

* **snow job** *n*. slang: An effort to deceive, overwhelm or persuade with insincere talk.

A curious development that offers an interesting perspective on the current state of the Japanese Mind is the eruption of vitriolic antagonism towards its mainland rivals, China and Korea, that hit the headlines during 2005. Two comic books, depicting Chinese and Koreans as base, inferior peoples, became runaway best-sellers. One book, *Introduction to China*, portrays the Chinese as a depraved people obsessed with cannibalism and prostitution, stating with no factual support that prostitution now makes up 10 per cent of China's gross domestic product. It also questions the veracity of Japan's worst wartime acts in China, including the Rape of Nanking in 1937–38, when as many as 300,000 Chinese were killed. A woman of Japanese origin issues this damning verdict: 'Take the China of today, its principles, thought, literature, art, science, institutions. There's nothing attractive.' Similar comments are made about Korea in *Hating the Korean Wave*. A report in the New York Times[19] discussed the offensive content of the two books, complete with unflattering drawings of Japan's Asian competitors, in the context of Japan's renewed xenophobia against two countries it has always regarded as inferior.

The paper quotes Kanji Nishio, a scholar of German literature and honorary chairman of the Japanese Society for History Textbook Reform. Mr Nishio, who wrote part of the book on Korea, is presented as a man who not only believes in bending the historical truth to present a certain picture of Japan, but is unyielding about the need for Japan to cut itself off from the two countries he seems to despise: 'Currently we cannot ignore South Korea or China. Economically, it's difficult. But in our hearts, psychologically, we should remain composed and keep that attitude.'

Japan's near-neighbour China, however, confronts quite different circumstances. The early 21st century will be seen as the era of China's corporate explosion, which has burst upon the world at unsurpassed speed. When Hampden-Turner and Trompenaars published their study of business cultures in 1993[20] the name of China did not even appear in the index. In the space of a decade all that changed as China, with its rapidly expanding industrial economy, joined the business big league. In 2005 came the first-ever Chinese attempt to acquire a major US enterprise when the country's state-owned oil giant CNOOC announced a $18.5 billion takeover bid for California-based oil company Unocal. The reaction of US politicians and media was as hostile and chauvinistic as French opposition to Pepsi's takeover plans for Danone. And it was no one-off. In August of that year Huawei Technologies made a $1 billion approach to acquire once-great British enterprise Marconi. It followed the acquisition by Lenovo, China's biggest computer maker, of IBM's personal computer division and Haier Group's move to buy Maytag Corporation, a leading US appliance manufacturer and owner of the legendary Hoover brand.

The rather bizarre scenario of state-owned companies founded in a communist state building a growing stake in the world's most capitalist economies is a pointer to the unpredictable shape of international corporate politics in the years ahead. A key factor shaping that future landscape will be the surge in Chinese economic power. On current trends China will reach about half the per capita income level of the United States by the year 2050, while its projected population of some 1.4 billion will be about 3.4 times the US population of about 400 million. At that point China's economy would be about 75 per cent larger than that of the United States – a towering colossus overshadowing the global economy and devouring its resources at an alarming rate.

China represents perhaps the most contradictory of all modern business cultures. Despite its Marxist heritage, the country has its own breed of corporations and their scale and global reach is growing by the month. Many of them are quoted on the world's leading stock markets, though behind them stands the might of the Chinese state. The top five have combined revenues of more than $150 billion and bear testament to the mix of old and new sectors – smokestack and high-tech – that characterises China's 21st-century business structure. Of that five, two companies are in oil and gas, two in telecoms and one in insurance.

But that is where any connection with the rest of corporate tradition ends. From a Western viewpoint, oriental business cultures seem to be the same, but they are not. Although Japanese companies are considered to have left behind their reputation for simply reproducing ideas originating elsewhere, they are in truth very good copiers and improvers of other people's work. The Chinese, in fact, are the innovators; it is simply that any free-wheeling inventiveness has been stifled by the monolithic political culture constructed by Mao Tse-tung and his successors. While Japanese business accords relatively low priority to financial rewards – Japanese CEOs are paid a fraction of their counterparts in other business cultures – Chinese society revolves around money and superstitions about wealth-creation. No Chinese company serious about success would ever include the number 4 in its corporate identity or brand descriptors; the number 8, on the other hand, is revered as the bringer of good fortune.

Exhibit: Business China – Magic Words & Numbers

Doing business among China's corporate community involves navigating a psychological minefield of numerological and linguistic folklore, much of it founded on profound superstition. As a result, things are never quite as they appear. Numbers and words overlap and collide in a kaleidoscope of obscure meaning: choose the wrong combination and your business prospects could be doomed.

Take numbers. In English, we use numerals as an unambiguous reference to quantity. For the Chinese they possess parallel associations; feng shui and numerology are closely related and numbers are regarded as having a magical quality of their own. Numbers represent the five elemental forces of metal, wood, water, fire and earth. They are often used to predict the future. For these and other reasons, numbers have a particularly powerful role in Chinese business thinking.

For example, the number 4, when pronounced, can mean something innocuous like 'world' or 'generation'. But it can also mean 'death'. The number 24 sounds like 'easily dying' and 2424 is to be avoided at any cost. The H.J. Heinz marketing department may be interested to know that their brand promise of '57 Varieties' is not good news in China. Five sounds the same as 'nothing' or 'no', while seven has the same sound as 'certainty'. And besieged bosses at troubled Levi Strauss should reflect on the fact that their flagship brand of jeans, the classic 501, fails the same test: the number means 'no unity'.

On the other hand, the number 6 is auspicious because it is twice 3, and 3 is regarded as a lucky primary number because it takes a minimum of three points to create a geometric shape; it is seen as the beginning of all things. Therefore 6 means 'progress' or the doubling of everything you started with. The two numbers 66, meanwhile, would sound the same as 'smooth running' – ideal for branding a car or motorcycle. The three-digit number 666, despite its satanic flavour, is also popular with the Chinese. The greatly coveted number 8 sounds similar to the word for 'prosper'. Within the framework of yin and yang, 8 (being an even number) also ranks highest on the yin scale and is associated with potential and growth. The combination 888 sounds the same as 'business will easily prosper'. On the other hand, 999 is not a desirable number because it is too yang and the only way for it to go is down. In China's pre-communist days 9 was reserved for the emperor; the doors to the Imperial Palace were decorated with 81 (9×9) doorknobs to signify the emperor's majesty. Unfortunately, history tells us the number did not save him from a sticky end.

So any visitor to China will be struck by how often the number 8 turns up in the telephone number for airlines, hotels and corporate offices. Chinese telecoms companies and car registration authorities are known to charge a premium for every number 8 they hand out to new customers. Just take a spin through the Shanghai telephone book. The Shanghai Shi Mao Riviera Garden Estate has managed to secure the number 6888 8888. And the Ritz Carlton Portman Hotel has a number ending with 8888, as does the Holiday Inn Crowne Plaza, the Sheraton Taiping, the Ocean Hotel and China Travel Services.

In like manner, if you take the lift in a Chinese high-rise building, you will invariably find there are no floors numbered 13 or 14. Lack of the first number may be due to the almost universal aversion to the unlucky 'baker's dozen'. The absence of 14 is easier to explain: as pronounced it sounds the same as the word for 'accidents'. If your car carries a licence plate ending in 84, you're likely to be given a very wide berth by other motorists; this numerical combination has the same sound as 'have accidents'.

Quirks of the Chinese language can also create serious problems for foreign brands planning to do business in the region. Among the large Chinese communities in South- East Asia the phrase for 'Volkswagen' translates as 'fortune is the root of disasters'. Ford, on the other hand, comes over as 'extra fortune'. Japanese electronics brand Aiwa strikes it really lucky: in Chinese the word means 'love China'. One Thai company involved in a joint venture with a Beijing state enterprise concocted a corporate name that meant 'pain in the back'. The company ran continuous losses for years.

Chinese business thinking draws on historic experiences vastly differently from those of Western corporations, including the legacy of Confucian and neo-Taoist philosophies, as well as a unique history of development. And though the excesses of the Cultural Revolution launched by Mao Tse-tung in 1966 were an attack on bureaucracy and university intellectuals intended to 'purify' Chinese communism, it could not purge the country of its deep historical inheritance. Maoist bureaucracies that have seeped into the business organisations of present-day China borrowed their frameworks, systems and inspiration directly from pre-communist Imperial administrative practices. These influences led to the creation of a network-based economy built on basic, personal concepts such as 'trust' rather than the impersonal legal institutions and contractual agreements that are the hallmarks of Anglo-Saxon corporate transactions. They also help explain important differences that separate the Chinese communist model from its former Soviet counterpart and make China's corporate environment unlike any other in terms of ethics and psychological bias.

But the rise of corporate China is only the latest chapter in the Second Dominion story. The years ahead will also see India become an economic powerhouse, with its own home-grown corporate community flexing its muscles on the world stage. In this sense, business history is turning full circle. In the early 19th century the two biggest economies on Earth were China and India.

The return to prominence of China and India will simply add further to the immense financial power that is accumulating under the control of a very small number of people in a few hundred corporate boardrooms around the world. By the closing years of the 20th century 51 of the world's biggest economic entities were corporations, not nations. Even though the vast majority of employers are small businesses, the world's 500 biggest companies control over 40 per cent of the planet's global wealth. On current trends, the 21st century could see the lion's share of the world economy fall under corporate ownership. In this way the Second Dominion has made corporations the arbiters of our collective future. For this reason alone it is essential that we understand the complex mosaic of the differing psychological factors that drive their conduct – the good, the bad and the so-far undetected.

WHERE ARE THE CORPORATE GOOD GUYS?

Whatever their national, cultural and philosophical differences, corporations have one important characteristic in common. They are all products of human endeavour, invariably the result of tireless efforts by one or two individuals with a pioneering vision and a boundless commitment to winning. They are extensions of the human mind and over time develop an organisational psyche that reflects the environment that has fostered them. Yet despite their burgeoning power most were slow to recognise that alongside the power and influence they were accumulating they had a parallel duty to behave as decent corporate citizens. Corporate 'missions' that appeared to put community and moral values first were common to the language of companies in every business culture, from the United Kingdom and United States to France, Germany and Japan. But there was invariably a deep divide between the moral mission and the money-making realities of the business.

Holiday Inn, for example, in its early days had a spirit driven by the strongly religious beliefs of its senior management. The company had a rule that in each of the 200,000 bedrooms in its system a Bible must be open on the dresser and its pages turned each day by the chambermaid. Compliance with this rule was enforced by the company's Senior Staff Chaplain, the Rev. 'Dub' Nance, who boasted of the countless errant husbands who had been saved from committing adultery by the sight of the opened scriptures. He even sold a Holiday Inn Worship Kit for $299 that included lectern, altar cloth, gold cross and electric candlesticks. As Martin Page recounts: 'Vice-Chairman Wallace Johnson confers with God about the company's affairs before leaving for the office every morning. He told me that he stands in his bathroom and puts his questions to the Lord "loud and clear".'[1] But Johnson's Mormon attachments were not allowed to interfere with the serious business of generating profits. While Holiday Inn expected its executives to consume modest quantities of liquor, even in their leisure hours, this taboo did not apply to the customers of its 1500 hotels.

But this is a tiny part of the picture of how companies frame their behaviour. Experience of the 20th century tells us that corporations generally did nothing voluntarily to make themselves better citizens. One major reason for not doing anything is that they did not have to. While individual conduct has long been governed by comprehensive social and legal frameworks, the rules of corporate behaviour have grown in a haphazard, patchwork fashion, invariably in belated response to some scandal, scam or consumer pressure. In essence, the corporation – certainly in its Anglo-Saxon embodiment – has been required by law to rank its stockholders single-mindedly above all other considerations, including personal misgivings. English company law, for example, states: 'The director(s) have a duty of care to the shareholder(s) of the company to act in the company's best interests even where doing so might come into conflict with their own personal interests.'

True, the past century was punctuated by efforts to soften the corporate tone under a 'good guy' mantle. Joel Bakan describes the 'New Capitalism' that appeared in the United States around the end of the First World War, when returning soldiers demanded a better deal from Big Business.[2] Major corporations such as Kodak, Goodyear and Standard Oil spent time and money projecting themselves as benevolent and caring, with better health, welfare and education programmes for their workers. Similar efforts were seen during the 1930s, when many people blamed the Great Depression on boardroom greed and poor management. In the United States, Supreme Court Justice Louis Brandeis labelled corporations 'Frankenstein monsters' capable of evil acts. In response, boardrooms embraced corporate responsibility. But it was little more than an outer disguise. Many business leaders reviled the New Deal announced by President Franklin D. Roosevelt in 1934 and a small group of them even considered a plan to overthrow Roosevelt's government.

In more recent years boardrooms have addressed a comprehensive range of issues. Environmental impact, product safety, employment conditions, relations with the customer and boardroom pay have increasingly challenged the bullying, do-as-I-please outlook of old-style companies, expressed in the immortal phrase of the first Henry Ford: 'You can have any colour so long as it's black'. But these nods in the direction of good corporate citizenship were all too often cosmetic; the business and its bottom line still came first. When managers talked of building a more relaxed, creative or inclusive 'corporate culture' they thought mainly in terms of how such a culture encouraged efficiencies and innovation and drove marketing and sales – things to do with the operational characteristics of the enterprise. In most boardrooms the concern was not for a healthier corporate persona, but a healthier balance sheet.

As a result most corporate boardrooms grew increasingly out of step with the realities of the marketplace, where consumer attitudes were undergoing a radical shift. In much of the industrialised world the long economic boom of the 1980s and '90s created unprecedented popular affluence. Paying for basic life necessities was becoming less of a priority; consumers were increasingly free to experiment and explore with their spending, to consume for fun. By the end of the 20th century the business challenge was about how best to deal with customer concepts driven by factors totally new to the management task: human emotions, imagination, desires, adventures, wants, dreams. As depicted in Rolf Jensen's *The Dream Society*,[3] in today's emotional marketplace people want products and services that match their lifestyle and values and allow them to live out their personal aspirations through how and what they consume. They no longer buy products and services for utilitarian reasons of practical usefulness and price. They buy the 'stories' behind the brand – watches linked to a sense of adventure, sunglasses associated with celebrity, cast iron stoves steeped in rustic values that allow the suburban buyer to escape the urban rat-race, at least in the mind. Just as important, these 'stories' have to be backed by a corporate personality they like and admire, a personality that reflects the dream.

The Art of Corporate Denial

It is here we encounter the central problem. This shift towards the emotional marketplace – Jensen's 'dream society' – caught many corporations unprepared. Though the sociology of their marketplace has changed dramatically, their underlying behaviour is too often still shaped by the ideas of a generation of post-war management gurus who showed little interest beyond the profit and loss account. Many of those gurus echoed the writings of the 18th-century Scottish thinker Adam Smith, author of *The Wealth of Nations* and generally regarded as the founder of modern economics, or the work of Frenchman Henri Fayol. But whatever the differences in their intellectual heritage, the gurus have preached pretty much the same sermon and their influence has persisted until today: corporations are there to produce wealth.

Not for nothing was Smith's economics dubbed 'the dismal science'. Central to his thinking was the belief that the corporate wealth-creating machine is exactly that – an unfeeling, impersonal machine governed by rules drawn from physics and mathematics, not by a desire for truthfulness. The secrets of corporate success would spring from better handling of the machine – managing production lines, spreadsheets and cash flow charts, sales and marketing campaigns, assets and liabilities. Success or failure depended on how well these mechanical factors were managed. As John Argenti put it in his study of corporate collapse: 'Five internal ratios are important. These are working capital, retained earnings, current profits, sales and market value as a ratio to debt. These all contribute to Z, which indicates a company's propensity to fail.'[4] The bean-counter language betrays an outlook that has little time or space for the dreams, emotions and desires of today's *Dream Society* consumer, or for honest behaviour.

Unlike Lillian Gilbreth and other early analysts of organisation behaviour, who gave value to invisible, qualitative elements in the workplace equation, the 'mechanical' school of management writing saw around them a world of quantifiable processes that could be measured and planned at the physical level, without heed paid to intangible human factors that could not be touched or counted. This belief in the mechanical rules of business was to have profound implications for how the behavioural patterns of modern corporations evolved and has left many of them psychologically ill-prepared for the quite different challenges of business in the 21st century.

There is, meanwhile, an important flip side to the emergence of the emotional marketplace. The radical change in consumer attitudes described above, which is really about what consumers *want,* has also rubbed off on how people will increasingly view the companies they buy from. They are developing an instinct for sensing the psychological buzz of a business and can quickly decide whether they like it or not. To the 21st-century aspirational consumer, products and services are seen to reflect the 'soul or spirit' – the psyche – behind the brand. To attract this new consumer, that soul or spirit must be shaped by acceptable standards of corporate conduct – standards that have very little to do with financial numbers but everything to do with a healthy soul.

This shift by ordinary consumers away from a focus on the tangible balance sheet towards 'good guy' companies was amply illustrated by the outcome of the Millennium Poll, the biggest ever survey of global public opinion about the changing role of companies, published on the eve of the year 2000. Based on interviews with 25,000 'average citizens' across 23 countries on five continents, the poll asked what these global citizens wanted from companies in the century that lay ahead. The results were extremely instructive:

- In forming their impressions of companies, people around the world now focus on citizenship values rather than financial factors.

- Two-thirds of those surveyed said they wanted all companies to go beyond their historical role of making a profit. They want companies to contribute to 'broader societal goals' – in other words, to be good guys.

- When it came to large corporations, in all but two of the countries covered by the study the majority of respondents wanted big corporations to 'go beyond' the traditional definition of the corporate role. 'Good conduct' factors such as honesty and fair play for employees featured way ahead of making a profit.

Source: *The Millennium Poll on Corporate Social Responsibility*
Environics International, December 1999

Put simply, the millennium generation want their companies to behave like nice people. Above all, they want them to mean it. Unfortunately, many companies are a long way from accepting the new realities, despite half a century of growing consumerist politics and increasingly well-informed public opinion. Since the breakthrough work of Ralph Nader in taking on the US automobile industry – and winning – with his 1965 book *Unsafe At Any Speed*,[5] a growing fraternity of special-interest groups has evolved, collectively demanding that business faces up to its wider social obligations. The pioneering Greenpeace, founded in 1971, Friends of the Earth and a host of consumer groups, publications and watchdog websites are just a sample of the immense counter-culture that has built on Nader's lead, dedicated to exposing corporate excess and making companies honest, better behaved and more accountable. To judge from the record, though, progress in the corporate truth game has been limited. Too many corporations have consistently indulged in massive denial about the impact of their activities on the wider community.

In practically every recent example of questionable corporate conduct there has been a glaring gap between the company's avowed commitment to responsible, ethical business practices and what it is actually doing in the real world – the essential definition of corporate bullshit and clear evidence of a warped psyche. With Enron and comparable scandals the result was total meltdown. Others have lived to bullshit another day. Although they all insist they have cleaned up their act, the jury is still out as to whether a leopard can indeed change its spots.

Four examples from our corporate casebook offer valuable insights. The conduct during the 1990s of two US corporations, ExxonMobil and Philip Morris, offers much food for thought. Both stories have been widely covered by the media and consistently feature in the activist campaigns of special-interest groups. Communities and individuals still suffer from the consequences of their actions; legal ramifications still keep the courts busy. The facts are pretty well known, though disagreements over interpretation still abound. Another oil company, Shell, provides a different perspective on what its critics say is a mismatch of promises and performance. The fourth example is from a seemingly more benign sector – cosmetics. The Body Shop always presented itself as an anti-Big Business green warrior, the planet's friend and an eco-friendly guardian of its customers' well-being. How well did this stand up to scrutiny? And what are we to make of the sale of Body Shop to the mammoth French cosmetics company L'Oréal? First, let us consider our two case studies from the oil industry – ExxonMobil and Shell.

Oil on Troubled Waters

'We pledge to be a good corporate citizen in all the places we operate worldwide. We will maintain the highest ethical standards, obey all applicable laws and regulations, and respect local and national cultures. Above all other objectives, we are dedicated to running safe and environmentally responsible operations.'

Source: ExxonMobil corporate website

Years on from Nader's assault on unsafe automobiles, long-established global corporations still repeatedly fail the 'good guys' test. Among the worst offenders have been companies in the petrochemical, tobacco, pharmaceutical and food sectors. Despite growing demands for corporate truthfulness, they have been consistently accused by a wide range of critics, victims, pressure groups and official bodies of lies, cover-ups, legal strong-arming and denial of the scientific facts.

One instructive case study is how Exxon (now ExxonMobil) has handled two major assaults on its reputation. The first was the catastrophic oil spill involving their single-hulled crude oil carrier *Exxon Valdez* in 1989. The facts are well known: 11 million gallons of crude poured into Alaska's Prince William Sound after the tanker ran aground. Some 1300 miles of shoreline and vast numbers of wildlife were affected in the worst marine spill in US history. The disaster prompted the US Congress to pass the Oil Protection Act and demand that all US tankers be double-hulled by 2015. The US Coast Guard estimated that had the *Exxon Valdez* been double-hulled – like a Thermos flask – this leakage could have been cut by around 60 per cent. The vessel's captain, who had stood down from the bridge and left a relatively inexperienced navigator in charge, was found to have alcohol in his blood. On top of a $50,000 restitution payment he was sentenced to serve 1000 hours of community cleanup service.

From the start Exxon worked overtime to shift the blame away from the company – in fact, to the Almighty. Exxon USA called the event 'an act of God' linked to human error. While there is no doubt that the captain's behaviour contributed to the disaster, it was only one factor in a wider pattern of corporate policies, including cuts in personnel, time pressures on their captains and continuing reliance on cheaper, single-hull tankers like the *Exxon Valdez*, that created a climate in which accidents could occur without the need for Divine intervention. The report by the Alaska Oil Spill Commission into the causes of the spill concluded: 'The grounding of the *Exxon Valdez* was not an isolated, freak occurrence but simply one result of policies, habits and practices that for nearly two decades have infused the nation's maritime oil transportation system with increasing levels of risk. The *Exxon Valdez* was an accident waiting to happen ...'

The *Exxon Valdez* story is of a company apparently so intoxicated by a cocktail of misperceptions and delusions about the true facts that all sense of reality went out of the window. According to Dennis Kelso, then Commissioner of Alaska's Department of Environmental Conservation, ExxonMobil's statements following the spill seemed so preposterous that he believed the only explanation was that they were 'part of a deliberate misinformation campaign'.[6] This view was supported by marine scientist Professor Rick Steiner, who believes that ExxonMobil 'constructed its own "reality" of the spill – minimal impacts and rapid recovery'.[7]

As if these blandishments were not sufficient, the company attracted great ire in subsequent years by continually appealing against a court-imposed $5 billion compensation package for communities damaged by the spill. It has also been accused of funding research in legal and academic journals that supports the company's argument that juries are not competent to rule in punitive damage cases like that of the *Exxon Valdez*.[8] On the tenth anniversary of the disaster a coalition of activists calling itself 'the truth squad' pressed US federal regulators to block the proposed ExxonMobil merger until the company paid up.

It is difficult to unravel exactly how much of ExxonMobil's expression of innocence for the spill is a practical effort in damage-limitation and how much is self-delusion and denial that springs from a dysfunctional corporate psyche. But it is noteworthy that some years after the Alaska disaster, under different leadership, ExxonMobil came under attack again, this time for refusing to accept arguments about global climate change, attempting to block legislation designed to tackle its causes and opposing the UN-supported Kyoto Protocol aimed at reducing greenhouse gas emissions.

The UN body concerned with developing climate change policies has made clear that the oil industry has a direct responsibility for tackling global warming, especially in the United States: 'Fuel combustion in domestic transport accounts for 20% of total greenhouse gases in developed countries. ... in the US transport sector emissions are projected to rise by 46% up to 2020.'[9]

But ExxonMobil's Chairman and CEO, Lee Raymond, chose to differ. During his tenure as boss of the company, which ended in 2005, he supported President George W. Bush in rejecting Kyoto and went on record with the observation: 'We do not now have sufficient scientific understanding of climate change to make reasonable predictions and/ or justify drastic measures ... Some reports in the media link climate change to extreme weather and harm to human health. Yet experts see no such pattern.'[10] In a repeat of their policy of funding research into issues around oil spill compensation, the company has also poured millions into think tanks and lobby groups that cast doubt on the facts about global warming. Deadpan company officials have admitted, with no sense of irony, that Mr Raymond 'sometimes pays a price for telling it like he sees it'. According to Ken Cohen, ExxonMobil's vice-president of public affairs: 'Honesty and directness are virtues. But they can also lead to scrutiny and attack.'

Case Study: The 'Science' Exxon Preferred to Deny

'We in ExxonMobil do not believe that the science required to establish this linkage between fossil fuels and warming has been demonstrated.'

Lee Raymond, Chairman and CEO ExxonMobil, June 2002 – in a speech to the 7th Annual Asia Oil and Gas Conference in Kuala Lumpur.

What of the 'science' that Exxon boss Lee Raymond refused to accept? There are masses of studies, reports and speeches on the issue of fossil fuels and global warming, all pointing to the same conclusion. Of particular relevance here are two studies commissioned by Friends of the Earth in 2003 from independent specialists on the contribution of ExxonMobil itself to the world's carbon dioxide emissions since 1882, when the company operated as the Standard Oil Trust. As the years passed, the company's contribution to carbon dioxide emissions steadily grew. By 2002 the company was producing 2800 million barrels of oil a year; the resulting emissions would amount to 298 million tonnes of carbon dioxide annually.

The studies maintained that over the period 1882 to 2002:

• emissions from oil sold by ExxonMobil totalled 20.3 billion tonnes of carbon dioxide

- seven of the top ten years for its emissions were after 1996, the year in which the Inter-governmental Panel on Climate Change (IPCC) Second Assessment Report found 'a discernible human influence on global climate' (the IPCC is a UN-backed panel of some 2500 independent scientists)

- 65 per cent of the company's emissions have been since the 1971 Study of Man's Impact on Climate conference of leading scientists reported a danger of serious global changes caused by humans

- concentrations of carbon dioxide are now substantially higher than at any time in 420,000 years; the current rate of increase is higher than at any time in 20,000 years

- the company now accounts for 5 per cent of the world's carbon dioxide emissions

Source: Friends of the Earth, '*Exxon's Climate Footprint*', January 2004

In terms of a diagnosis, what we are looking at here is something that at first appears to be a massive case of corporate denial. But we must be careful to distinguish between denial and lies. Liars mean to lie; they know the difference between lying and telling the truth. Denial is something else; it is associated with guilt or fear, but it is not always a conscious process. We need to separate 'subconscious' from 'conscious' denial – whether or not you actually know you are denying something. Put another way, denial is about being careless – to a greater or lesser extent – as to whether something is true or not, while a liar deliberately sets out to misrepresent the truth. You could say ExxonMobil is aware of the truth on these issues but has a huge investment in disputing the facts. We have to ask what such a pattern of corporate denial tells us about the health of a company's underlying psyche. The bigger the corporation, the bigger is their vested interest in supporting their own theories about external realities. To take a more extreme case from recent history, the Nazis needed to 'prove' their prejudice against the Jews, so they concocted an entire master race theory to justify their anti-Semitic policies.

A major challenge for ExxonMobil was how long the company could keep up this policy of 'honesty and directness' about climate change now that not only top scientists but influential US politicians were speaking out on the growing dangers of the greenhouse effect. In August 2005 Presidential hopefuls Democrat Hillary Clinton and Republican John McCain and California Governor Arnold Schwarzenegger went on the record with strong statements accepting the case for global warming. Clinton and McCain are reported as saying that the evidence of climate change has become too stark to ignore and human activity is a major cause.[11]

Meanwhile, in September 2005 former President Bill Clinton launched the Clinton Global Initiative to deal with key world challenges, including climate change. The opening sentence of the CGI statement of aims says: 'Human beings are changing the Earth's climate. Around the world, heat-trapping gases from human activities are raising temperatures, changing rainfall patterns and altering the length of seasons. These alarming trends threaten livelihoods and long-established ways of life in every nation.'[12] Governor Schwarzenegger was more blunt: 'The debate is over. We know the science. We see the threat posed by changes in our climate.'[13]

As with the Alaska spill, ExxonMobil again chose to exonerate itself from responsibility. With the Alaska spill one could at least argue that bad luck played a part alongside a litany of corporate practices inviting disaster. But the same cannot be said about the debate on climate change, where an overwhelming body of scientific opinion points to a serious and escalating problem directly linked to the burning of fossil fuels. More than that, research suggests that ExxonMobil heads the list of villains.

There is an interesting historical footnote to this tale of corporate 'honesty and directness'. Standard Oil was created in 1863 and was the bedrock of the Rockefeller family fortune. It was ordered to be broken up in 1911 by the US Supreme Court under anti-trust laws. As a result some 34 separate companies were spun off. One of them was later named Esso, in homage to Standard Oil's acronym – SO. In this sense the spirit of the judicially disbanded Rockefeller empire lived on behind the mask of a clever wordplay. The Exxon brand was created for the US market in 1972; the Esso name is still used in many overseas countries. Another company became Mobil, to reflect the mobility revolution that reshaped America after the rise of popular motoring in the 1920s. One of the other spin-off companies was not so aptly named. Humble Oil was re-branded as Enco – for Energy Company. The name was swiftly dropped when it emerged that in Japanese it translated as 'stalled car'!

Although Exxon and Mobil both grew separately into vast billion-dollar global enterprises, US anti-trust agencies did not deem them big enough or powerful enough to block their remarriage in 1999, despite the efforts of 'truth squad' activists. So Standard Oil was once again reconstituted, like two long-separated halves of the same corporate soul. Today it has more assets than any other corporation on Earth. It is also the world's most profitable company and vies with one or two other corporate giants for number-one slot in terms of market capitalisation. Its annual revenues of more than $275 billion exceed the GDP of Indonesia, a country with a population of more than 240 million.

Shelling Out the Truth

Though not comparable with ExxonMobil's habit of maintaining that the Earth is flat, Shell also has been accused of projecting a corporate voice that is at variance with its true self. The heritage of the company stretches back over a hundred years and has origins far removed from the rough-and-tumble macho world of oil rigs, refineries and supertankers. In 1833 Marcus Samuel opened a small shop in London selling sea shells; Victorians used them to decorate trinket boxes and the like. The business quickly grew into a thriving import–export company. A few years later, during a visit to the Caspian Sea to search for new shells, Marcus's son spotted an opportunity of exporting kerosene oil for lamps and cooking to the Far East. Cargo ships were chartered, the kerosene business flourished and the Shell oil company was born.

Today, as part of Royal Dutch/Shell, the company is ranked as the fourth-largest corporation in the world, with annual revenues of $270 billion. With its business activities focused on extracting, processing and transporting natural resources, Shell has inevitably been at the sharp end of the environmental debate. For decades it has attempted to reinforce its green credentials through good works. Its film unit and motoring guides fostered a benign image of a company that reached out to the community. More recently its corporate advertisements have carried messages of environmental responsibility and a caring outlook. As the company's website put it: 'The aim of the campaign is to tell Shell's business story and position ourselves at the heart of the energy debate. We feel that only by behaving responsibly can any company hope to operate profitably.'[14]

Unfortunately, events over the years have revealed a glaring gap between promises and reality. The most celebrated incident is the massive public outcry in 1995 that followed the discovery that Shell planned to 'decommission' the massive Brent Spar oil storage buoy by towing it from the North Sea and dropping it in the Atlantic. The decision, as it happens, was backed by a great deal of respected scientific opinion. The disposal plan had been approved by UK Prime Minister John Major, while a letter to *The Times* from experts at the Institute of Oceanographic Sciences commented that sea disposal was 'probably correct'. But Shell's decision struck a deeply abrasive chord with environmental campaigners, who quickly provoked damaging headlines around the world. Greenpeace activists abseiled onto the facility from a helicopter while the huge buoy was being towed and sent live footage direct to TV news networks. Greenpeace press statements – later found to be inaccurate – took Shell to task for threatening the oceans with toxic pollutants. In Germany, where Shell has considerable business interests, a gas station was fire-bombed and petrol pumps boycotted.

Brent Spar illustrates how badly the company had misread public opinion over an issue it considered safe territory. The incident highlights the danger of sheltering behind corporate mantras about environmental values that are very difficult to deliver in an industry based on invading

Nature's integrity. Despite technical inaccuracies in the Greenpeace arguments, the incident stirred a powerful emotional response and the company was forced into an embarrassing U-turn. In an effort to present a more eco-friendly environmental profile Shell withdrew from the Global Climate Coalition, a lobby group set up to fight green campaigners on global warming, and declared itself committed to sustainable development. It also supports the International Labour Organization's Declaration of Principles and Rights at Work. These days its publications and corporate website devote much space to promoting the company's ethical credentials.

But all the declarations and principles in the world cannot argue with the facts. And in its environmental record Shell has found it very difficult to back words with deeds. One telling example is the evidence that came to light in 1996 – a year following the Brent Spar affair – that the company had been polluting a huge underground water reserve in Turkey for some 25 years. Greenpeace maintained that leaked internal documents showed that Shell had pumped over 480 million barrels of production water contaminated with crude oil, solvents and other chemicals into the Midyat aquifer between 1973 and 1994. Midyat is near the city of Diyarbakir in southeast Turkey where up to 2 million people live.

Greenpeace concluded that Shell knew it was polluting the aquifer and had set aside funds to reduce the problem. The company subsequently stopped this work and sold the operation to Perenco, a company specialising in extracting further revenues from mature oilfields. According to Greenpeace, one leaked memo states: 'It is unfortunate to see a change of priorities towards maximising cash before divestment by sacrificing environmental targets.'[15] If these documents are correct Shell managers must have known the injection into the aquifers was against both EU and Turkish environmental regulations.

Case Study: Green Delusions?

How far has Shell delivered on its publicly avowed commitment to responsible behaviour? Brent Spar and the Midyat aquifer story date back to the mid-1990s. What since? In April 2003 Friends of the Earth decided to put the company's record across the world to the test. In their report *'Failing the Challenge'* they took up Shell's offer of a dialogue on its corporate conduct. The report was based on personal statements from people with first-hand experience of living next to Shell's activities. These statements were verified by independent auditors.

Here is a flavour of their findings:

• 'Behind the glossy brochures and inspiring sound bites about working with people and for the environment we have found that Shell continues with many of its old ways.'

• 'Shell is attempting to cultivate an image of a company that takes climate change seriously. But the company has not, as yet, translated its concern into action. Shell has not ceased or scaled back its exploration or production activities. On the contrary, it is expanding wherever possible.'

• 'Communities living near Shell refineries, pipelines and oil spills as far apart as Texas and North West China have accused the multinational of jeopardising their families' health, impoverishing their quality of life and shortening lives.'

• 'Shell can't be said to have embraced sustainable development in anything but words.'

• 'Hazardous sites are always near black and coloured communities. It's South Africa's historical blueprint.' [16]

The report brings together witness statements and comments from communities close to Shell facilities – in most cases communities that were there long before the corporation moved its operations into the area. In Port Arthur, Texas, there are stories of routine emissions that many link to the high incidence of cancer, asthma and other respiratory diseases amongst the local population. 'Up to 80 per cent of people have breathing difficulties and heart conditions.' Similar reports come from people around Shell installations in Louisiana.

Along Nigeria's Niger River Delta oil spills and gas leaks, the report says, are a common occurrence, due in large part to the corrosion of old pipelines. Shell's involvement in the Tarim Basin gas fields in North West China, being developed by the company to help fuel booming economic regions in the east of the country, has gone ahead amidst accusations of social and environmental degradation and human rights abuses. In the Philippines a Shell-operated complex near Manila is cited as having a long history of oil and chemical leaks, pollution and fires affecting local communities. Respiratory infections, skin diseases and other conditions are rife. In 1999 a pipeline running through a heavily populated district ruptured, burning 325 homes and killing a local resident. In the same year, a Shell oil tanker collided with another vessel in the mouth of the Rio de la Plata off Buenos Aires. Some 16 kilometres of riverside were polluted and a wildlife area designated by UNESCO as a biosphere reserve was devastated.

The report concludes: 'Shell tries hard to cultivate an image of a responsible multinational. It spends millions on glossy brochures and advertising to convince us all – and perhaps itself – that it is a leader in corporate and social responsibility. ... The real life stories in this report suggest senior management should spend less time on the message and more on making a difference.' [17]

According to Friends of the Earth, Shell managers declined to comment on the report.

Problems of a different kind surfaced in 2004 when Shell announced the company had booked inflated oil reserves in previous years. The ensuing reserves downgrade accounted for nearly one-fifth of the company's 'proven' oil reserves – at the time the largest ever reserves re-categorisation for any oil company in the world. Shell was subsequently fined over $140 million by US and British regulatory authorities. *Business Week* later reported that a leading New York law firm, brought in to investigate, painted 'a devastating portrait of Shell as a dysfunctional company where the two top executives ... were on increasingly hostile terms'. The magazine quoted one executive as writing to the other: 'I am becoming sick and tired of lying about the extent of our reserves and the downward revisions that need to be done'.

The reserves scandal dealt a hefty blow to Shell's corporate reputation and raised questions about the company's corporate governance and compliance procedures. It also brought into sharp focus the wider issue of Shell's 'good guy' credentials. Should we be convinced by those reassuring corporate advertisements about caring for the planet and its inhabitants? Effectively, Shell are saying 'We are green. We are compassionate.' But are they really? It might be better if Shell stuck to emphasising the virtues of their industry and stressed the benefits we enjoy from having oil. In effect they should be saying: 'If you want your fridge, your car and so on, you need us. Because we do all the dirty work – the refining and the rest.' A sensible approach would be to run an advertising campaign featuring a giant oil rig surrounded by a host of products and everyday activities that oil makes possible.

But this is diametrically opposite to what the company is doing. Many would regard those 'green' corporate advertisements as a dishonest, even seriously unethical, public information campaign. Shell would be better advised to come clean: 'Yes, we screwed up the planet. But now, for charitable and strong marketing reasons, we are putting something back.' After all, the main motive for Shell in all this is to protect the company's bottom line. And it certainly has been a success here; it is Europe's most profitable corporation.

The key consideration is the degree to which Shell's strategy threatens the future of the business. The company seems to follow a slightly deluded assumption that says 'We can mislead you.' By and large, if you lie to yourself, you will be the prisoner of a delusional perception. With this comes a risk that you build a delusional world in which corporate decision-making becomes erroneous.

Ifs and Butts

For many years 'the science' didn't trouble the tobacco giants, either. And they recruited some of the best brains in the advertising business to help them sleep at night. While ExxonMobil was busily fending off an angry public, cigarette producers like Philip Morris – once dubbed by *Business Week* 'America's Most Reviled Company' – were testifying at a Congressional hearing in 1994 that nicotine was not addictive and was not a drug – views totally at odds with the opinion of government and independent scientists (and probably most of their smoking customers). This testimony was delivered exactly 30 years after the US Surgeon General issued his first official report accepting the health risks of smoking. At the time of the hearings the Surgeon General and the American Medical Association estimated that cigarettes were killing over 400,000 smokers every year. James W. Johnston, Chairman and CEO of RJ Reynolds, questioned this figure, saying the estimates of death 'are generated by computers and are only statistical'. This same tobacco industry testimony refused to commit itself on whether smoking caused cancer or heart disease.

A closer look at the story reveals a long-entrenched industry habit of delusional linguistic sophistry and double-talk designed to sidestep the argument on smoking and health. Since the World Health Organization has recently reported that approximately 100 million people died over the course of the 20th century from 'tobacco-associated diseases'[18] – a figure expected to rise sharply over coming decades – this must be the most extreme case of head-in-sand corporate denial on record.

Among the best reporting of this case study is the investigative journalism of Pulitzer Prize-winner Alix M. Freedman, who covered the story for the *Wall Street Journal*.[19] Freedman alleges that an internal cigarette company document likens nicotine to cocaine, which if true indicates a sharp difference between the tobacco industry's public utterances and confidential documentation produced to inform its internal debate. This internal–external dichotomy is a prime marker of gold-plated corporate bullshit.

Key allies of the tobacco companies in their battle to deny consumers the unpleasant facts were, of course, the major advertising agencies, who deployed an array of psychological weapons to keep their customers onside and attract new ones. At those same Congressional hearings RJ Reynolds boss James Johnston apologised for an advertisement for their Camel brand that recommended that young men seeking dates at the beach drag women from the water, pretending to be saving them from drowning. Perhaps the best known instance is the use of a rugged cowboy to sell Marlboro cigarettes by conveying the image of an open-air, independent, even rebellious individual at ease with Nature – a man who won't be bullied and makes his own choices.

Exhibit: The Inside Dope About Ciggies

The history of tobacco advertising is a veritable theme park of fact, fiction and downright lies. In this conspiracy of corporate dishonesty, the advertising industry must share responsibility with the big-spending clients that helped make them rich. Even the most cynical observer will feel impelled to congratulate advertising agencies over the years for their clever manipulation of the psychological foibles of the consuming public. But what does the historical account tell us about the psychological condition of tobacco companies and the agencies that have conspired with them to con people into dicing with death?

Before the 1930s the health problems associated with cigarettes were unknown and never discussed. Indeed, during the 1920s, cigarette advertisements in the United States often claimed to be 'doctor recommended' and 'good for digestion'. One slogan read: 'For Digestion's Sake – Smoke Camel.' But scientific awareness was beginning to build. In 1932 the American Journal of Cancer carried a learned paper linking cigarettes to cancer, which triggered a wave of research and further papers highlighting health concerns about cigarette smoking. In 1951 the British researcher Richard Doll began a massive long-term study of 34,000 UK physicians which, by 1956, had already provided convincing statistical proof that smoking increases the risk of lung cancer. A turning point in public perceptions was an article published in 1957 in the mass-readership *Reader's Digest*. By 1964 the US Surgeon General entered the fray with an official report connecting smoking with cancer, based on more than 7000 scientific papers on the issue.

The initial reaction of the tobacco industry was to question the validity of the research. The 1953 Annual Report of Philip Morris, for instance, carried the comment: 'At one time or another within the past 350 years practically every known disease of the human body has been ascribed to the use of tobacco. One by one these charges have been abandoned with the realisation that they were not tenable.' [20]

But as the debate gathered force, the industry, concerned by the potential impact on popular perceptions and therefore sales, moved towards the concept of the 'healthier' cigarette, in particular the adoption of filter tips. In 1952 only 1.3 per cent of cigarettes had filters. Pretty soon they all had. By the 1970s the industry moved on yet again to what became the 'Tar Wars', with companies competing for the lowest tar cigarette. But the real shift in the approach of the cigarette companies was in the psychological tactics they adopted to persuade people to light up. Advertising campaigns moved their focus away from the main area of public concern, the act of smoking itself, to build totally unconnected associations in the minds of consumers.

But the running battle for the psychological high ground – if that is quite the right term – took agency creative teams ever further along the route towards the ultimate in playing impenetrable mind games with the smoker. One especially zany press advertisement for Marlboro cigarettes featured what looks like a corrugated iron shack on a storm-swept ranch. It is raining heavily and a thick stream of rainwater is pouring off the guttering into a large oil drum. This is what one bemused commentator had to say:

'Marlboro ads generally focus on one or both of two key themes, namely sex and anxiety/death. Allied with both of them there is a secondary theme, that of oral activity. As any mature individual knows, smoking is an oral activity. Sex can also involve oral activity. The present ad seems to be advocating both oral sex and death. One theme might give pleasure, the other ultimately tends to produce pain and suffering as well the makers of Marlboro cigarettes know. Even those who smoke and view the ad know this in their heart, hence the various connotations that can be derived from consideration of the water barrel and the "pissing" drainpipe. The ad makers could be "taking the piss" out of their clients. They could be intimating that smoking is like "pissing in a barrel" in that you never get complete satisfaction from a cigarette.' [21]

Meanwhile, a look at the evolution of the Marlboro advertising campaign reveals how cleverly it adjusts to changes in the prevailing public debate. In 1964, when the health argument was still very new, we see Marlboro Man unashamedly lighting up. By the 1970s the cigarette is featured in the hand, as an accessory. By 2000 there is no cigarette in the picture at all, just a lone cowboy. A similar thing happens to the cigarette pack. In the '60s and '70s the box figures prominently, at first shown separately on a white background then gradually integrated into the picture. By the 1990s the Marlboro box has either disappeared altogether or been reduced in size to function more as a logo. And throughout, the product is sold without reference to its purpose as a nicotine delivery system but instead as offering a benign sensory pleasure in the manner of fresh asparagus or cherries: 'Come to where the flavour is.' [22]

An interesting twist on the Marlboro story is that the adoption of the 'Marlboro Man' cowboy to give the product a rugged, macho profile was a radical departure from a prior tradition of soft-selling the very same brand. The company had introduced Marlboro into the US market in 1924 primarily as a women's cigarette – many years earlier it enjoyed great success in Victorian England as a 'mild as May' women's smoke. Meanwhile, history records that the real-life cowboy who played the Marlboro icon in a long advertising campaign, Colorado Springs rancher Bob Norris, lost both his parents (who were lifelong smokers) to emphysema. Norris was also a close friend of Hollywood legend John Wayne – a chain smoker who died of cancer in 1979. Naturally, this information did not appear in any of the product's advertising campaigns.

An equally revealing aspect of cigarette advertising is how the big tobacco companies blatantly harnessed historical events and political trends in the early years of the 20th century to recruit more women smokers. This was to take the art of psychological deceit into totally new territory. With each shift in socio-economic dynamics an appreciation of prevailing social nuances was put to work to attract new women consumers and generate higher sales. Again, US advertising agencies led the way.

In the late 1920s and early 1930s the cigarette was adopted by American women factory workers and college students as a symbol of rebellion and independence – ironically the same mix of associations behind the adoption of Marlboro Man. Tobacco companies targeted this promising new market with campaigns specifically crafted to appeal to feminine sensitivities. One campaign for Lucky Strike, for example, urged women to stroll along New York's Fifth Avenue during the Easter Parade, holding cigarettes to represent 'torches of freedom'. In case this psychological ploy failed, the product was also promoted as a way of losing weight. The slogan read: 'To keep a slender figure, no one can deny. Reach For a Lucky Instead of a Sweet.' Given the consensus on the potentially lethal consequences of smoking, the idea of a selling a cigarette as a weight-loss mechanism has an especially macabre ring.

During the 'feminist' years of the 1960s and '70s, cigarette companies attempted to cash in by creating 'women's brands'. The Philip Morris campaign for Virginia Slims, for example, relied on aesthetics and emotional connections to shift product. The Virginia Slim cigarette was thin, narrow and white – an obvious appeal to women striving to replicate the same attributes. The ads themselves featured – you guessed it – attractive, skinny, fashionable young women alongside the congratulatory slogan 'You've Come A Long Way, Baby.' In subsequent years the Virginia Slims campaign was revamped to reflect the multicultural world created by the rise of professional working women with senior jobs in banking and law, global travel and the Internet. The slogan now was 'Find Your Voice', accompanied by pictures of seemingly empowered, independent women from different ethnic backgrounds smoking cigarettes. Yet again, the advertising copywriters seem to have missed the irony of their strap line: the last thing you will be able to do after a hard night out on the cigarettes is find your voice.

The tobacco industry has proved itself extremely adept over the years at finding the right words to suit differing occasions. It has skilfully used language to build false realities about its products and create imaginary worlds for its customers to inhabit – not smoke-free but certainly free of self-guilt. It even developed ways of kidding itself that nasty things never happen in the tobacco business. One instance came to light during court hearings in the US State of Minnesota in December 1994, the same year 'Big Tobacco' gave its controversial Congressional testimony. The State, along with health insurance organisations, had instituted proceedings against major tobacco companies, including British American Tobacco (BAT). Court documents lodged by the State included the following claim: 'By 1957, BAT researchers were using the code name "zephyr" for cancer. For example, in a March 1957 report, BAT stated: "As a result of several statistical surveys, the idea has arisen that there is a causal relation between zephyr and tobacco smoking, particularly cigarette smoking."' In real life the word zephyr means 'gentle breeze'.

Case Study: Smoke and Mirrors

During the 'Big Tobacco' debates of the 1990s Pulitzer Prize-winning journalist Alix Freedman constructed a comprehensive catalogue of tobacco industry porkies designed to present a public case that was in stark contrast to the unpalatable truths circulating within cigarette companies themselves. Key allegations made by Freedman were as follows:[23]

• In April 1994 William Campbell, President and CEO of Philip Morris, testified before a congressional hearing that 'nicotine contributes to the taste of cigarettes and the pleasures of smoking. The presence of nicotine, however, does not make cigarettes a drug or smoking an addiction'. Alongside him, giving similar testimony, were the most senior executives of six other companies that together comprised America's 'Big Tobacco'.

• Over the ensuing months company whistleblowers began leaking internal documents out of the tobacco corporations to politicians and the media. In December 1995 Freedman ran a series of articles in *The Wall Street Journal* about the discrepancies between their congressional testimony and confidential company memos and reports.

• One internal draft report allegedly produced by an employee of Philip Morris opined that cigarettes are a 'nicotine delivery system' that people smoke to get nicotine into their bodies and that nicotine is chemically 'similar' to drugs like cocaine.

• This same draft report also refers to a proposal for a 'safer' cigarette known by the code name 'Table'. Apart from the usual resort to linguistic games, by talking about a 'safer' cigarette the industry is, of course, acknowledging the perceived dangers of the ones it is designed to replace.

• Jack Henningfield, chief of the pharmacology branch at the US government's National Institute of Drug Abuse said the draft report was a 'blunt recognition of what public health scientists have been saying all along'. A nicotine research specialist at the University of California said: 'This sounds like an excerpt from the Surgeon General's report.'

• In a hurried damage-limitation exercise Philip Morris spokesman Steven Parrish attempted to spin-doctor the draft report: 'We have acknowledged in public documents that nicotine, like many, many other things, has pharmacological effects, but that doesn't mean that cigarette smoking is addictive. This document nowhere says that nicotine produces addiction.'

• Freedman returned to the story a few weeks later. This time he drew on two documents he maintained were major internal reports by Brown & Williamson Tobacco Corporation, one of the seven congressional testifiers.

– The reports described how cigarette producers allegedly used chemicals such as ammonia that enhanced nicotine delivery to the smoker by scavenging nicotine from the rest of the tobacco in the cigarette.

– They also threw serious doubt on industry claims that smokers were attracted to a 'rich aroma' or 'pleasure' or 'satisfaction'. Quite simply, they were hooked on nicotine.

– B&W were especially interested in how Philip Morris's flagship brand Marlboro had established its commanding position in the market. Their internal documents affirmed their belief that the ammonia-rich filler used in Marlboro delivered a 'nicotine pick-up potential'. The manufacturing technique was adopted by other tobacco companies.

Here, too, we see a good example of the denial-versus-lying issue, much the same as in the case of ExxonMobil. It would appear that Philip Morris was engaged in a form of conscious denial. But the kind of posturing described here has a far simpler explanation, one of a sheer commercial necessity to cloud the facts about the wholesomeness of their products. It is important to understand that being psychologically flawed in some way does not also require you to be dishonest about it. Individuals can be honest about their dysfunction: 'I am into sado-masochism.' They do not have to pretend that they are not. But selling products deemed by an overwhelming body of scientific opinion to be dangerous is not about honesty, it is about a lustful desire to conquer markets.

In January 1998 the US cigarette industry changed its script. Senior tobacco industry executives testified before Congress that nicotine is addictive 'under current definitions of the word' and that smoking 'may' cause cancer. Such was the level of public hostility generated by its previous campaign of denial that the Philip Morris corporate persona was comprehensively revamped, including changing the parent company's name to Altria. The word is not a million miles from 'altruism', meaning 'regard for others'. The company says its new name is derived from the Latin word *altus*, meaning 'reaching ever higher' – an even more intriguing take on the business of selling products widely recognised as giving the user a 'high' and whose deleterious health risks are beyond dispute.

The new Altria website boasted of the company's Compliance and Integrity programme – 'a critical part of our commitment to responsible business conduct'. The company's Chairman and CEO, Louis C. Camilleri, is quoted as saying: 'Our commitment to integrity must always come first.'[24] In the wake of this corporate personality transplant a senior officer with Philip Morris, David I. Greenberg, wrote of the dangers of corporate wrongdoing: 'Rule bending is contagious. In no time it can burrow deep into an organisation's culture. The result is often a full-blown epidemic.' Some would describe that as the voice of experience. Meanwhile, it remains to be seen how long the company's muddled 'Altria' revamp, with its confusing and over-complicated mosaic logo, survives in a business sector that will increasingly demand a straight-talking, bullshit-free relationship with its consumers.

Your Body or Your Soul?

Case studies in corporate conduct come in different shapes and sizes but none can match that of a company that embraced the very highest behavioural and ethical standards, grew to global status and then spent years fighting off accusations about hollow promises and empty mission statements. Oil companies can be in no doubt about the true nature of their business. Tobacco giants know, deep down, that inhaling smoke can never be a formula for robust health. But what of the seemingly benign world of face creams and eye shadow?

The Body Shop was launched in a small shop in Brighton in 1976 with the help of a £4000 loan from a friend. At the time, Britain's high streets were dominated by traditional retailers with dusty, tried-and-tested product ranges. Body Shop was different. Its founder, Italian-born Anita Roddick – who was made a Dame in the Queen's Birthday Honours List in 2003 – targeted Britain's hippie counter-culture market with a range of 'natural' body care products and grooming services that included 'one-stop' ear piercing. She offered 25 different kinds of products in five differently-sized bottles that could be refilled – a radical concept at the time. Anita and Body Shop hit the bullseye. Customers were more than happy to buy products they considered natural, high quality and backed by an ethically driven business philosophy. In time there were 2000 stores in 51 markets operating in 25 languages.

Body Shop presented itself from the start as a switched-on, eco-friendly alternative to established high-street brands. The company's first mission statement promised that Body Shop 'will be the most honest cosmetics company in the world'. During the 1980s Roddick broadened its 'green' mission by connecting with social causes such as animal testing and AIDS awareness. Her most significant association was with the issue of endangered rainforests, in particular with the Kayapo people in Brazil, from whom she sourced small amounts of nut oil for use in her hair conditioners. Roddick was soon transformed into a campaigning powerhouse and the scourge of governments and corporations that neglected their environmental responsibilities. She would be spotted in 1999 on the front line of anti-globalisation demonstrations during the 'Battle of Seattle' that protested against the World Trade Organization and the evils of Big Business. Media pundits dubbed her 'The Mother Teresa of Capitalism'. The company promised it would 'try to ensure the business is ecologically sustainable, meeting the needs of the present without compromising the future'. And, lest cynical observers missed the point, Body Shop senior management made clear the company's aims 'are not just fads or marketing gimmicks'.[25]

But Roddick's elevation to the business sainthood had a major downside. She and the company soon fell under profound scrutiny from journalists keen to expose flaws in her apparently squeaky-clean image and commitment to natural products. In 1994 the American investigative journalist Jon Entine published an article called 'Shattered Image: Is The Body Shop Too Good To Be True?' in the US magazine *Business Ethics*. In it Entine wrote about what he calls 'the gap between Roddick's rhetoric and the Body Shop's practices'. The article, an edited version of a longer investigation that was refused publication, was subsequently accorded a National Press Club Award.

Body Shop was soon confronted by an ever-growing literature questioning not only the verity of its green manifesto but, more vitally, its claim to be 'the most honest cosmetics company in the world'. One former senior colleague is reported to have described Roddick as a 'myth-o-maniac', while a noted cosmetologist suggested the company should be renamed the 'Shoddy Bop'. Ten years after Entine's investigative piece was spiked his original article was published in full in *Killed: Great Journalism Too Hot To Print*, a collection of stories stifled by editors.[26] It paints a powerful picture of what Entine believes are dramatic contradictions between Body Shop International's idealistic public image and its real-life operations – a core characteristic of corporate bullshit.

Case Study: Anita's Dysfunctional Coffin

'To tirelessly work to narrow the gap between principle and practice, whilst making fun, passion and care part of our daily lives.'
Body Shop Mission Statement.

Enlightened business writers share the view that prolonged success is often the major cause of eventual decline – the so-called Icarus Paradox. The story of Anita Roddick and the Body Shop she founded offers another perspective on the idea: believing your own, self-generated, rosy publicity, while comforting to the believer, can seriously damage your future commercial prospects. Many successful companies attract negative publicity, for a huge variety of reasons, and yet still go on to prosper. But this particular case study raises a quite separate issue: was this seemingly delusional tendency also a manifestation of underlying psychological problems that could undermine the longer-term commercial prospects and independence of the company?

Let us examine the record. In its early days Body Shop could do no wrong. It matched the consumer mood of the time. It garnered massive free publicity extolling its fresh and green attributes.

Over the years Roddick constantly reminded people that she had 'never, ever paid for a single page of advertising'; the Body Shop's reputation did all the work. It opened stores on every continent; eventually there would be some 2000 outlets across the world.

When the company was floated on the London Stock Exchange investors flocked to buy. Body Shop developed the reputation as 'the shares that defy gravity'. At its peak in 1992, 16 years after launch, its share price reached £3.72 and the company was worth £700 million. But in the years that followed, all the green philosophy on the planet could not stem the steady erosion of customer and investor confidence in the Body Shop story. The Roddick formula began to be seen by market watchers as increasingly tired and complacent. Established high-street cosmetics brands, for so long trailing Body Shop's worthy, eco-friendly appeal, had reformulated their product offer and began to claw back market share in the space Roddick had monopolised for years. Consumers found there were better-priced alternatives, environmentally responsible and of comparable or superior quality, a few stores down the road.

In 1998, amid reports of shareholder pressure, Anita Roddick stood down as CEO and was replaced by Patrick Gournay. But hopes that Gournay would lift Body Shop's spirits and its share price were short-lived. In 1999 the company announced 300 job cuts at its Sussex headquarters after business results deteriorated sharply. In the year to February of that year earnings had collapsed by 90 per cent. The job losses were designed to cut costs and 'improve the group's ailing performance'. Buyers for its manufacturing plants in Littlehampton had been found. The situation in the company's 'troubled' US operations was 'disappointing'. The company board admitted it had got it wrong over the crucial Christmas trading period, 'with an offer that wasn't strong enough'.

Body Shop limped on through the fallout from the dotcom bust. In 2001 the Body Shop share price fell to a low of 91 pence, a quarter of its peak value. In a speech in Edinburgh that year Roddick described Body Shop as a 'dysfunctional coffin'. In 2002 Patrick Gournay left the company. Market commentators mused about possible buyers of the business. The commercial problems continued; in 2003 the company's shares touched a low of 56 pence.

Then something very bizarre happened. In April 2004 Body Shop began a three-year, £100 million global investment programme as part of a radical new strategy to move away from its hippie roots and target older and wealthier consumers. Company documents describe Body Shop's new brand as 'masstige' – a market positioning somewhere between mass market and prestige aimed at women 'who seek function and indulgence'. In the company's refurbished shops the old dark green box disappeared. Instead, there were sleek glass counters that gave them the air of an expensive-looking boutique. Out had gone the trademark black-topped bottles and the range of container sizes that so attracted young, budget-conscious customers back in the '70s. The new, luxurious Spa Wisdom range would not be out of place in the Harrods beauty hall.

In March 2006 this transition seemed complete when Body Shop was bought for £652 million by the French multinational giant L'Oréal, a price tag almost £50 million lower than the company was worth in the early 1990s. Dame Anita Roddick was reported to have made about £130 million from the sale. She described the deal as 'the best 30th anniversary present the Body Shop could have received'.

But the takeover by the world's biggest cosmetics company raised many eyebrows. L'Oréal, which has annual revenues of $18 billion, is 27 per cent owned by the Bettencourt family; Liliane Bettencourt is listed by *Forbes* as France's richest resident with a fortune worth $17.2 billion. Her father Eugène Schueller, who founded L'Oréal in 1909, was an alleged Nazi sympathiser who financially supported a violent French fascist-leaning group known as *La Cagoule*. Her husband, former French Cabinet minister and one-time Deputy Chairman of L'Oréal, André Bettencourt, wrote anti-Jewish articles for a German-financed newspaper during the Occupation.

At the time of the Body Shop acquisition L'Oréal's worldwide advertising campaign centred around the strap line 'Because You're Worth It'.

The takeover by L'Oréal raises wider questions about maintaining the innate integrity of a company that built its brand around 'small business' values and social causes. But this story is really about a company that lost touch with its marketplace, but never noticed until it was too late. Its 'masstige' strategy – not exactly a reflection of the company's hippie heritage – may have succeeded, but analysts doubt whether Body Shop as an independent company had the financial resources to carry it through. And the signs from the marketplace were hardly encouraging: in January 2006, on the eve of the deal with L'Oréal, shares in Body Shop slumped by 20 per cent after disappointing Christmas sales in Britain and the United States.

From the standpoint of its corporate psyche the commercial problems that built up for Body Shop over recent years – and helped make the company vulnerable to takeover – can be explained by a failure to register the changing consciousness of consumers and a major shift in broader economic realities, not least in the company's home market. When Anita Roddick launched the business in the 1970s Britain was in dire economic distress and consumer attitudes were shaped by utilitarian needs. Thirty years later Britain was the world's fourth-biggest economy, with levels of popular affluence to match. Body Shop's response was to stick to the company's original business formula. In time its outlets began to look tired and irrelevant. To use a very basic comparison, one could liken them to a pretty girl dolled up in bloomers, when every other girl at the party is wearing thongs. As with Levi Strauss, with their belated efforts to jazz up their apparel with a few stick-on designs, Body Shop metaphorically added flowers to the bloomers in the hope of making them more sexy. But it was not enough; Anita's Earth Mother message had become seriously out of step with a new fashion spirit best summed up in the slogan: 'If you've got it, flaunt it!'

The L'Oréal deal apart, the growing barrage of criticism and counter-claims made Body Shop the focus not only of investigative researchers but of academics drawn to the moral conflicts raised by efforts to run an ethically-driven business in a tough competitive world. Some refer to what they call 'the myth of good intentions'. As for the people who work for the company, there are issues here, too. Body Shop's pay levels for its store staff over the years have invariably challenged prevailing standards on what constitutes a decent wage. On awkward issues like employee representation, the company made it clear that 'Body Shop does not formally recognise any Trade Unions as representing its employees.' It remains to be seen how the company will develop, and what promises it will make, as part of the world's biggest cosmetics corporation.

4

THE DISHONESTY PANDEMIC

ExxonMobil, Shell, Philip Morris and Body Shop are, of course, among the more heavily publicised stories of corporate bullshit at work. Less visible to the public eye have been thousands of other episodes where company conduct was widely at variance with its own professed values of good corporate citizenship. But at least they did not cross the line that divides the disingenuous from the downright illegal. That, however, would change with the flood of corporate crimes and misdemeanours that straddled the turn of this new millennium and strengthened a popular belief that corporate 'good guys' are hard to find – and probably always will be.

Some will argue that the behaviour of the oil majors and 'Big Tobacco' was typical of the corporate old guard with their psychopathic ways and that you would never catch the new breed of post-1960 baby-boomer business start-ups going off the rails in this way. Certainly, the founding 'soul and spirit' of ventures like Body Shop and Ben & Jerry's was characterised by social mission and crusading zeal – although both, ironically, are now owned by multinational giants. Another new breeder, Virgin Group's Richard Branson, became renowned for spurning corporate convention by wearing neither jacket nor tie. And it was noteworthy that established computer giants like IBM would be challenged by a perky new arrival that took its name and logo from a fruit. In contrast to the *Matrix*-like character of IBM, with its strict dress code, short hair rule and serious countenance, Apple Corporation – born April 1976, the same year as Body Shop – presented a cheery, dress-down image of a company where work was fun.

Such companies seemed to reject the values of the corporate old-timers and traded on the growing public preference for caring, sharing businesses with a New Age slant. Branson would tell journalists that his long-range business plan was simple: 'We take on the big bad guys.' The mission of Apple, said the company, was 'to give every individual the ability to do their best'. These companies represented a fresh approach to corporate culture, with a laid-back business style and an often spiritual demeanour. Most important of all, they seemed to represent a break with the tradition of huge, rapacious conglomerates busily consuming the world's riches. They seemed to give business a good name – at least on the surface. But, in truth, are they good guys?

Certainly, many of these newcomers burgeoned and profited handsomely by stealing the moral high ground from the old guard. With the business agenda shifting to the invisible side of the corporate balance sheet, old guard management strategy, heavily focused on the mechanics of business operations, was being left behind. Company mission statements began to express green values and fluffy, people-friendly visions. Annual reports became catalogues of sponsored good works and 'inclusive' principles that avowed respect for the needs and rights of all stakeholders. Advertising campaigns promoted not only product qualities but the company's community virtues. Top executives ran sponsored marathons in support of charities. Companies everywhere took to funky HQs, 'dress-down' Fridays, flexi-hours and employee share options. By all appearances, business was becoming benevolent, ethical, responsible and honest.

And this is where the apple begins to rot. While companies have been busily jumping onto the bandwagon of corporate nice-ness, they have not addressed the most crucial issue of all. As with an individual, corporate appearances are only skin deep. If 'good guy' actions are nothing more than corporate bullshit intended to mask a corporate persona that is still driven by ingrained 'bad guy' habits, there is a serious gap between observed conduct and psychological realities. This is the core characteristic of a dysfunctional organisation – a 'psychotic' company – where words and actions and underlying personality traits are in conflict. The lesson of human psychology is that a dysfunctional entity rarely succeeds in achieving its chosen goals.

In one scenario this could mean a company afflicted by self-delusion of the kind that drove Enron to catastrophe in 2001, when billions of dollars disappeared into a black hole. We need to remind ourselves that Enron was also a young start-up, no more than 16 years old when it hit the skids. But it is unclear just how far the rot has spread throughout the global corporate community and still lies undiscovered. As this book illustrates, corporate appearances are usually deceptive. Enron's rapid rise to commercial greatness, for example, was applauded by investors and business commentators alike and its senior executives lionised for their seemingly unparalleled managerial skills. For their part, Enron's partner-in-crime Arthur Andersen had long been universally regarded as the gold standard name in global auditing.

Case Study: Behind the Mask

The corporate scandal that best defines the 'dishonesty pandemic' of recent years has to be Enron. This energy trading company rose in 16 short years from nowhere to become the seventh biggest enterprise in the United States, with 21,000 employees in over 40 countries. In October 2001, two months before it went under, the company was valued at $28 billion. It was toasted on Wall Street and applauded by leaders of the business press. In 2000 *Fortune* awarded it the accolade: 'Enron – the most innovative company of the year.' In June 2001 *The Economist* declared: 'Enron has created what may be the most successful Internet venture of any company in any industry anywhere.' Meanwhile, top brains at the respected business consultancy McKinsey made public their verdict that 'Few companies will be able to achieve the excitement extravaganza that Enron has in its remarkable business transformation.'[1]

Enron was certainly innovative, successful and remarkable – but not in quite the way meant by its admirers. Behind the company's success was an elaborate scam that enabled Enron's board to present to the outside world a picture of corporate health that was, in truth, a pack of lies. And while the scam disguised mounting financial problems, senior executives stuffed their pockets with millions of dollars and transformed their corporate offices into an

Aladdin's cave of artworks and expensive furniture. The combined wages bill of the company's top 200 executives soared from $193 million in 1998 to $1.4 billion by 2000 – an average of $7 million each and in total about one-and-a-half times Enron's annual earnings. It was alleged by the US Department of Justice that between 1998 and 2001 Chairman and CEO Kenneth Lay received about $300 million in stock options, on top of $19 million in salary and bonuses. He cashed in the options, netting a profit of over $217 million. To brighten up their work surroundings Enron's in-house art committee was given an acquisition budget of $20 million.

Enron could not afford this profligacy but deployed an elaborate system of financial deception – with the support of its then-respected auditors, Arthur Andersen – to cook the books and cover up the grim truth. It also cheated on its responsibilities as a corporate citizen. Using complex tax schemes – external tax dodge advisers earned some $87 million in fees from the company – Enron avoided paying billions of dollars to the US government. Between 1996 and 2000 the company posted profits worth nearly $1.8 billion yet somehow managed to generate $381 million in US federal tax rebates. During this period Enron paid just $17 million in taxes – less than 1 per cent of its total profits.

After an intensive investigation of Enron's criminal deceit, the *Financial Times* reached a blunt conclusion about what it called 'a virtual company with virtual profits': 'Enron bolstered profits by booking income immediately on contracts that would take up to 10 years to complete. It shifted debts into partnerships it created and in effect controlled, even though defined by auditors as off balance sheet. It used such entities to manipulate its accounts at the end of each quarter and employed financial derivatives and other complex transactions aggressively to the same end. It masked poorly performing assets with rapid deal-making.'[2]

The fallout from Enron's collapse was far-reaching. Public sector workers across the United States, including teachers and firefighters, saw about $1 billion wiped off their retirement funds. Enron staff lost further billions after company shares they had been urged to buy by the company's senior management became worthless. The Enron share price fell from $84 to practically nothing in less than a year. But perhaps the biggest cost of all was the comprehensive loss of trust in corporate institutions provoked by the Enron scandal and the wrongdoing of scores of other enterprises across the world. In July 2004 Kenneth Lay was indicted by a federal grand jury on charges of conspiracy, securities fraud, wire fraud, bank fraud and making false statements

Equally costly in terms of public confidence was the demise of Enron's auditors, Arthur Andersen. The firm haemorrhaged staff and clients and, besieged by allegations of helping Enron falsify its accounts and shredding tonnes of incriminating documents, soon went out of business. With annual fees of $9 billion and 85,000 employees, Andersen was the world's leading audit firm and had a heritage and global presence far greater than that of Enron. For years it had been regarded as synonymous with the highest standards of professional conduct and had an unrivalled track record in corporate and social responsibility. It had audited Enron's accounts throughout that company's 16 years of existence, earning a total of $52 million a year in fees for a range of auditing and related services.

This landmark case study brings us to another key factor in appraising seemingly dishonest behaviour. When weighing up aspects of denial or lying the essential consideration is *intent*. Did the company have a deliberate *intention* to deceive? With Enron the most powerful driver of its conduct for most of its brief life was probably the intention to *succeed*. When the company ran into trouble this driver changed into an intention to *deceive*. The important thing is 'appropriateness': while wanting to succeed is an appropriate psychological condition, acting to deceive is inappropriate – and inappropriate emotions invariably create problems.

At the time, Enron's collapse was the biggest in US corporate history. But even this feat was surpassed when the $100 billion telecoms colossus WorldCom, as it happens the exact same age as Enron, went bust after investigators revealed a fraudulent cover-up relating to billions of dollars in hidden losses. Arthur Andersen, which was the auditor for both

companies, was this time convicted of criminal accounting practices
– a bizarre fate for a long-respected auditing name renowned for its
active role in teaching the principles of business ethics. It was as if the
whole of corporate America had embarked on a massive dishonesty
spree. Over a five-year period some 1200 US companies were forced to
restate their accounts.

But these scandals were not solely a US phenomenon. Indeed, the first
in this pandemic of mega-scandals struck in Australia, in 2001, when
the insurance firm HIH collapsed with debts of A\$5.3 billion – about
US\$4 billion. It was the biggest corporate collapse in Australian history.
Nine top executives were subsequently charged over company accounts
that had been generously massaged to show non-existent profits. HIH
boss Ray Williams, it was revealed, lavished thousands of dollars on
jellybeans, cigars and gold watches.

Taking the lead in Europe was the dairy products giant Parmalat, Italy's
eighth biggest company, which fell apart in late 2003 after massive
financial irregularities were uncovered. A €4 billion bank account of a
Cayman Islands subsidiary was found to be completely fictitious. The
company's founder and chief executive reportedly admitted siphoning off
€500 million into family businesses. The Parmalat accounts were found
to have a black hole in excess of €10 billion. The media dubbed it 'the
Enron of Europe'.

Case Study: Milking Billions

Parmalat was Italy's dairy giant – and a family company founded
and run by Calisto Tanzi (a university drop out), his brother
Giovanni and son Stefano. For 16 years Tanzi's finance director was
Fausto Tonna, described by one banker as 'a peasant in manners
but with an extremely sharp financial mind'. Like so many of our
cast of corporate characters, the company had humble origins, as
a small-scale seller of prosciutto in a tiny northern Italian village.
At its peak Parmalat employed 36,000 people and supplied long-
lasting and other milk products in 30 countries.

As with many of our case studies in failure, difficulties began when the company decided to expand overseas, with an acquisition in Brazil in the mid-'70s. Global growth was accompanied by an equally fast-growing debt mountain. In 1990 the company was bailed out but the Tanzi family were forced to give up 49 per cent of its controlling share. Not to be fazed by the obvious risks of overseas expansion, Parmalat in 1997 bought Beatrice Foods, a major US dairy products brand, before moving in to China, Australia and Mexico.

To the outside world, Parmalat had become an Italian corporate fairy tale – an obscure peddler of ham transformed in to a global colossus. But behind the scenes the real fairy tale was playing out – in the falsified accounts and secret offshore dealings designed to sustain a pattern of management dishonesty of epic proportions. An opaque system of accounting had been created using an elaborate network of some 130 financial institutions. In December 2003, Italian financiers were puzzled when the company had difficulty meeting a €150 million payment of a bond: Parmalat was believed to have cash reserves of nearly €4 billion. Calisto Tanzi dismissed it as 'a bit of a liquidity problem'.

Tanzi was being more than 'economical with the truth'. He soon admitted that the cash mountain did not exist; nor did the Bank of America account it was supposed to be sitting in. A letter from the bank sent to curious auditors in March 2003, confirming the account's existence, turned out to be a forgery. When investigators began probing into a tangled web of company finances they found that billions had either gone astray or had never existed in the first place. In all, the accounting calamity at Parmalat had prosecutors trying to discover what happened to more than €10 billion in vanished assets. Shares in Parmalat, once worth €1.8 billion, became worthless. In June 2005 Stefano and Giovanni Tanzi, along with former company employees and an external advisor, were found guilty of market manipulation by a Milan court. Calisto Tanzi was indicted separately and sent for trial. Also arrested were senior executives from leading banks and auditing firms.

Parmalat was Europe's biggest-ever corporate bankruptcy but was only part of a wider pattern infecting European business. In 2002 shares in the French media conglomerate Vivendi, also advised by Andersen, fell by a third after a report in national newspaper *Le Monde* that the company tried to flatter its 2001 accounts by as much as €1.5 billion. In 2003 the Dutch super-grocer Royal Ahold restated its earnings by $1 billion for the three years ending 2002; most of this was connected to an overstatement of earnings at a US subsidiary. The move prompted a 60 per cent drop in the company's share value. In December 2005 the company paid $1 billion to settle a class action lawsuit with shareholders.

Meanwhile, another case, that of Swiss staffing company Adecco, highlighted the growing nervousness afflicting European audit firms in the wake of Enron and other scandals. Adecco has entered business school lore as 'the Enron that never was' after a jittery auditor refused to sign off the company's 2003 accounts. Adecco shares took a hit as the company name was mistakenly ranked by regulators alongside Ahold and Parmalat and US law firms launched class actions on behalf of shareholders. Six months later the accounts were signed off without qualification: the original snag was linked to technicalities in the application of tough new US accounting rules. The episode generated 22 million pages of investigative documents and cost Adecco €100 million.

Japanese corporations by tradition follow a more socially responsible approach. But they, too, were rocked by a series of scandals at the dawn of the new century – though not in the same league as the massive financial misdemeanours seen elsewhere. As reported earlier, in July 2000 the country's leading dairy products brand was exposed for flouting hygiene rules and a sister company was subsequently caught disguising imported beef as home-grown produce so as to qualify for mad cow disease subsidies. A few weeks later it was discovered that a major Japanese energy generator had routinely falsified inspection records at its nuclear plants. Such episodes have eroded Japan's long-standing public faith in its business community.

Put simply, at the turn of the 21st century the rich industrialised world was overtaken by a seemingly universal breakdown in corporate honesty. The combined value of these corporate bankruptcies exceeded the gross domestic product of a medium-sized country. Although global in nature US corporations feature prominently in the list of wrongdoers. One possible explanation for this is the marked contrast between managerial incentives in the United States and those in Europe or Japan, incentives that place immense pressure on US bosses to perform, at any cost. A recent study points out that CEO compensation as a multiple of average employee compensation was 531:1 in the United States but only 16:1 in France, 11:1 in Germany, 10:1 in Japan and 21:1 in nearby Canada. Even the United Kingdom, with a system of corporate governance closely similar to the United States, had a ratio of just 25:1.[3]

Belatedly the authorities attempted to stem the tide, but they were as always several steps behind. Even so, the result was a tidal wave of tough new business laws that would saddle corporate boardrooms with a massive compliance headache and a new management climate that demanded transparency and truthfulness.

In the United States the reaction of lawmakers was uncompromising. As the pro-business *Fortune* magazine put it, the explosion of wrongdoing and dodgy accounting practices at Enron, WorldCom, Tyco, Qwest, Global Crossing, Arthur Andersen and other top US companies 'created a crisis of investor confidence the likes of which hasn't been seen since the Great Depression'. This crisis sparked a massive overhaul of US corporate law and the introduction of a draconian new regime through the Sarbanes-Oxley (SOX) legislation passed by Congress in 2002. Its provisions are regarded as the most radical overhaul of US business rules since the 1930s and a symbol of the total failure of the system to control the errant ways of powerful and rapacious corporations. In the words of one commentator: 'The 2002 Act was passed in response to almost daily reports of greed, corruption, fraud and opulence plaguing the top echelons of corporate America.' Under SOX, the penalty for certifying an annual report that is later proved to be misleading, for example, is up to 10 years in prison. If an individual 'wilfully' misleads, the penalty can be as much as 20 years in jail.

In Britain an equally rigorous approach has been adopted by the Financial Services Authority and other watchdog agencies, much of it pre-dating SOX by a decade. Alarmed by scandals at the Bank of Credit and Commerce International, the conglomerate Polly Peck run by Asil Nadir and the Robert Maxwell business empire at the start of the 1990s, a radical overhaul of the UK's regulatory machinery was undertaken years before fraud and corruption were uncovered amongst leading US corporations.

EU and Japanese regulators are also taking a hard line, though there are key differences of approach compared to the Anglo-Saxon regulatory model followed in the United Kingdom and the United States. In a parallel development, much of the industrialised world – outside the United States – is adopting single accounting standards that will add another layer of regulatory discipline. Known as International Financial Reporting Standards (IFRS), they will embrace some 100 countries, including EU member states. The United States has its own Generally Accepted Accounting Principles (US GAAP), which follow somewhat different guidelines.

Meeting these stringent new rules imposes a growing financial burden on corporate balance sheets – one report suggests that spending on IT and related services for compliance purposes could be as much as $3 million for each $1 billion in annual revenues.[4] Apart from the cost to individual companies – in 2005 Barclays Bank declared a $84 million charge for SOX compliance alone – the tough new regulatory climate places an unprecedented responsibility on management to behave honestly and openly at all times and requires companies to work hard to be good corporate citizens. This climate should encourage a culture of 'truthfulness' and the idea of 'the truthful enterprise', but old corporate habits die hard. Even so, though the global business environment is still far from achieving a truly transparent framework for corporate governance, the seeds have been firmly planted.

This culture of 'truthfulness' poses a powerful challenge to every 21st-century company and the people who run it. They must not only build a compliance culture that can meet unprecedented and growing regulatory demands, they must also foster good conduct in the boardroom and throughout the company's management structure. The truthful enterprise must become honest with itself about its strengths and failings – and open and honest with its marketplace. This includes a fresh approach to how it frames its promises to consumers and presents its personality to the outside world, with no more delusion or denial. It means cutting out the bullshit. As we have maintained throughout this narrative, all this can only be achieved in a lasting way if there is harmony between the company's stated intentions and the psyche that drives its behaviour. For many companies this will be a painful task. But for every business it is essential if it is to survive and prosper in the years ahead. In the new era of corporate honesty, papering over the psychological cracks is not an option. The psychotic company will always pay the price, sooner or later.

Part Two

IN SEARCH OF THE PSYCHOTIC COMPANY

5

COMPANIES ON THE COUCH

In this *third phase* of corporate evolution, where the condition of the corporate psyche is key, two intangible factors play crucial roles. Both are vital elements in building a winning business. The first factor is a *company's view of its own personality* – how it sees itself; where it wants to go and how it intends to get there; what it believes others think of it. If this mixture of perceptions is out of balance or lacks consistency and harmony, the company will tend to make inappropriate decisions about its business direction and is unlikely to succeed in fully achieving its chosen goals. It may fail to get out of a declining market and into a new and growing one. It may speak to its customers in misleading, outdated or irrelevant language. It may misunderstand the nature of a major competitive threat. It may choose the wrong target when planning a merger or acquisition.

Such failings explain the fate of many of those corporate names that dropped from the heights of greatness decades ago and no longer figure among the lists and indices of leading companies. In most cases, just as with people, the true psychological picture was usually obscured by words, actions or some other camouflage designed, intentionally or otherwise, to cover up underlying dysfunctions and project a favourable image to the outside world – the very definition of corporate bullshit. Thus, psychological insight into a company's persona is an essential first step in stripping away the bullshit and laying the foundations for a successful way forward. A company with low self-awareness may not project its future correctly and may stick with a personality model that is inappropriate. Many companies have fallen prey to this dysfunctional state and face difficult times in the years ahead.

The second intangible factor is a *company's behaviour*. This has several dimensions. In today's 'good guy' culture of corporate and social responsibility and transparency towards the consumer, 'behaviour' is a vital differentiator in setting apart those companies that gain public respect and support. Such companies have earned their 'licence to operate' in the consumer marketplace and stand a better-than-even chance of hanging on to it in the future. Companies that lose, or never fully acquire, that licence to operate will almost certainly die. Failure may come sooner if a company's ingrained habits of conduct lead it, say, to cook the books or pillage the balance sheet. Enron, Parmalat and WorldCom – all brought down by enormous financial scandals – are typical examples of this category.

Or problems may come later if an arrogant, negligent, complacent or uncaring outlook alienates or erodes customers' allegiances to the point where customers eventually switch their loyalty to a competitor. One well-known corporation, Levi Strauss, steadily lost market share to more innovative competitors and was forced to downsize to a shadow of its most successful self. The legendary jeans manufacturer could well be the Laura Ashley of the 21st century, trapped in the margins of a marketplace it once ruled. Another illustration might be Kodak, which created the popular camera and film market in the 1900s (its first Brownie models sold for just $1) and dominated it for generations. But Kodak fumbled the transition from traditional image technology to new digital opportunities and saw competitors like Fuji, Canon, Sony and Hewlett-Packard move ahead of it. Kodak has slipped in rank on the *Fortune 500* list from 43 in 1955 to 153 in 2005, while making regular announcements of earnings slippage, job losses and plant closures. In 2003 Kodak cut its dividend for the first time in 120 years.

We noted earlier that corporations tend to have an almost religious belief in their own immortality. As we have shown, this is far from the reality; there is a constant churn of corporate winners and losers and former leaders continuously disappear from the top rank, many destined for oblivion. Their place is taken by new entities. Some are amalgams of the old, where a stronger enterprise absorbs a weaker competitor or even several of them. These are invariably presented to the outside world as a 'merger of equals', with much talk of 'valuable synergies' that will carry the merged partners off towards a golden sunrise of open-ended profitability. This, too, is a good example of corporate bullshit: in almost every instance there is one dominant partner that imposes its culture and habits on weaker components of the resultant enterprise. If this dominant personality is also a dysfunctional one, the dysfunctional characteristics take over the new entity.

In a high proportion of such 'mergers' the weaker partners would have collapsed had they not found safe haven in the more substantial balance sheet of their suitors. Almost always their corporate identity – their name, logo and livery – disappears for ever. Sometimes both partners lose their identity; the formation of IT services company Unisys, for instance, saw both Sperry and Burroughs expunged from the corporate lexicon. And as for whether these 'partnerships of equals' offer a sound commercial proposition, here, too, there is a lesson from life. Corporate mergers are like marriages: they succeed or fail for exactly the same reasons marriages do. History suggests that corporate marriages have enjoyed about the same survival rate as the human variety. It all depends on whether two different personalities, with different psychological dynamics, can get along together.

Others of these new entities are start-ups based on some bright idea, a new customer proposition or a different business model applied to an existing market. The attrition rate among them is high, but those that meet new marketplace needs, target a shift in consumer mood or re-invent a tired, over-mature industry can rise quickly to a position of leadership or niche strength. Dell, easyJet and the UK-based soap retailer Lush are good examples of imaginative and energised entrepreneurs developing a totally new approach to a business sector that has been around for decades. And then there is the high-tech tribe – Google, Yahoo!, Amazon, eBay, QXL, lastminute.com and a host of other web-space ventures – that operate as virtual corporations, the vanguard of a vast population of online variations that will mushroom at an exponential rate as the 21st century exploits the infinite possibilities of the World Wide Web and its offspring. But despite their innovative cheek, bravado, chutzpah or sheer will to win, they are nevertheless all organisations, with perceptions and behaviours and a capacity to make inappropriate choices that could compromise their future.

Whatever their age and heritage, all companies conform to one of several psychological stereotypes, just like individuals. So the tools of psychological analysis can be applied to identify any conflicts or disharmonies that generate dysfunctional personality flaws in an organisation and threaten its survival. It is not enough to maintain a solid balance sheet or achieve greater efficiencies. Constantly appraising its own psychological well-being is an indispensable exercise for every company if it is to maintain and sharpen its competitive position. Yet despite the critical importance to top management of understanding the psychological condition of the business and that of its competitors – or of a supplier, commercial partner or take-over target – it is a seriously under-used practice. The most probable reason is that managers have never been expected to think this way.

Put crudely, company decision-makers must borrow from human psychology and regularly ask themselves a blunt question: 'In reality, is this company what it thinks it is and wants to be?' If a company fails to ask such a question, it will never know whether it has a false picture of its own personality – whether it surrounds itself with bullshit. If it does confront such issues it could unmask important underlying problems. But, for differing reasons, the typical enterprise never faces up to its demons. In the long run that organisation and its people may find themselves trapped in inappropriate behaviours and failure might not be far behind. Hence, companies need to assess how they are perceived – by themselves and others – as well as to assess their perceptions of their clients, their markets and their own history. They constantly need to adjust to change and address new developments, new competition and new market forces – things that are difficult to achieve if they don't have an honestly appraised picture of themselves.

Is This Really Me?

We can borrow from human psychology to produce a checklist of what constitutes a 'healthy' psyche. Psychologically healthy people exhibit most or all of the following:

- An objective perception of reality

- Acceptance of their own nature

- A commitment and dedication to some kind of work

- Naturalness; simplicity in behaviour; spontaneity

- Independence; a need for autonomy and privacy

- Intense mystical experiences

- Empathy with and affection for all humanity

- Resistance to conformity

- Democratic characteristics

- Keenness to be creative.

Not for nothing is the emphasis on having 'an objective perception of reality'. Without knowing who and what a company is all about, it is probably impossible to develop a future strategic vision that is sustainable, identify and seize upon new market opportunities or make emotionally appropriate business choices. Equally important, without having a thorough appreciation of the psychological make-up of your commercial rivals, it is unlikely that you will appreciate the nature of their competitive threat and be able to act to thwart it. Senior managers are universally familiar with traditional tools of analysis that help them plot corporate strengths and weaknesses, opportunities and threats. They spend countless hours devising future strategies based on a five- or ten-year vision and developing plans and measurement schedules to achieve those strategies. They strive to innovate and re-invent, to build teams and alliances with other enterprises. They invest vast sums on the technologies they believe can make that future vision a reality. But the most important task of all is left untouched: is this company psychologically equipped to deliver on those goals?

In our experience when this question is put to a typical board of directors the answers that come back are highly varied and usually not very insightful. Quite simply, they are not in the habit of thinking about the organisation in this way. This book departs from traditional management writing and offers some basic guidelines as to how they can develop such a habit. But applying it effectively calls for a level of honest appraisal that is woefully rare in the typical boardroom. When you ask those same directors how they think the company is perceived by others, often they will give answers that are simply not consistent with the business challenges they say they face. Indeed, the whole topic of corporate self-awareness is rarely considered outside the marketing department and even they may have a totally unbalanced viewpoint. How many marketing executives are prepared to admit that the company that employs them is afflicted by flawed personality traits? How many even think about such concepts?

We can look at the task of self-knowledge from three perspectives: internal, external and projected. The first poses the question: 'How does this organisation see itself?' The second asks: 'How does it think others see it?' The third asks: 'How does it wish to be seen?' The ideal state is where all three answers are the same – where everyone, inside and outside the company, shares the same viewpoint about what the personality of the enterprise is all about.

These exercises in perception analysis can be ranged against a core question: 'What does this organisation want to achieve – what is its future vision?' The answers to all of these questions provide the basis for a preliminary assessment of the psychological condition of the subject as a first step towards determining whether its perceptions support or obstruct its business goals. Further questions can help us to discover what makes a company move. How is success measured? How did the top people get their jobs? How do people communicate within the business? What are the intellectual and behavioural conformities? How do people speak and dress? How is the company seen by people in the same industry and by its suppliers and customers? How does the company behave in a crisis?

Honest answers to these questions are the starting point for gaining valuable insights and drawing up a psychological description of the company. This will characterise the predominant emotional forces and identify strengths and weaknesses – and possibly even pathologies, the symptoms of underlying problems. Above all, it will help in predicting what types of dysfunction could paralyse the business. To take one example, victims of the dot-com crash were invariably dysfunctional businesses run by business people overtaken by a manic optimism that led them to mis-read or ignore the threats to their survival – they simply thought they were fireproof and that success was inevitable. A similar tendency to overlook important signals of impending change explains why a bull market always overshoots and why bear markets become excessively risk averse irrespective of any optimistic market indicators; people seem to have an innate tendency to believe things will carry on as before, despite evidence to the contrary. The problem is quite basic: who or what in any organisation has the responsibility for managing such issues? Since no company has a 'Who-Am-I?' department, who is responsible for this very important job? If it is to be successful, the 21st-century enterprise will need to address this crucial topic.

But perceptions apart, the key focus must be on corporate behaviour. The way an organisation conducts itself – what it does and says – springs from its underlying psyche. The case of ExxonMobil, described earlier, offers many insights into a corporate psyche that seemed to foster denial and an instinct for rejecting blame for the consequences of its actions. Tobacco giant Philip Morris spent years refusing to accept its true nature as a purveyor of products that even millions of its customers recognised as being hazardous to their health. Laura Ashley and Levi Strauss long behaved as if their marketplace had remained unchanged from the heyday of their business success. General Motors chose to ignore the emerging competitive threat of world-class Japanese rivals – and is now seen by business commentators as bearing the early signs of becoming the biggest corporate basket case of the 21st century. IBM tells the world the future is in computing hardware – just as software is becoming the driving force of information technology. Sony refuses to recognise a radical shift in the global market for music, turns down the chance to acquire iPod technology – and cedes significant ground to Apple in a rapidly growing business sector. In every instance corporate behaviour reflects some inherent flaw in the psychological make-up of the organisation.

Apart from behavioural traits – what companies do and say – we can also tell a great deal about a corporate persona by observing the visible symptoms, signs and signals that betray the state of a company's psychological well-being. In earlier chapters we have looked at such things as logos, colours, numbers and even headquarters' buildings. We also need to take a critical look at how companies relate to their customers, hire their employees (and dress them), design their websites, as well as management training programmes, the style of the AGM, even the staff Christmas party – anything that offers a window into the subconscious of an organisation. Why does a company drag its budding talent off to Outward Bound courses to run across hot coals and brave white-water rapids? Or hire an expensive society photographer to shoot tasteful pin-up poses for its high-profile annual calendar? All betray important facets of the reality within.

IBM again offers an instructive perspective. For many years it required its male staff to dress within very conservative limits not unlike those required of Mormon missionaries. On one celebrated occasion the company sent home a legal executive for coming to work in loafers. It also expected its people to be acquainted with the company's corporate songbook. One song carried the lyrics: 'March on with IBM, We lead the way, Onward we'll ever go, In strong array; Our thousands to the fore, Nothing can stem, Our march forevermore, With IBM.' How much did this regimented and self-preoccupied ethos contribute to IBM's mounting business woes during the 1980s? When the company headhunted Louis Gerstner in an effort to save the company after it posted a $8 billion loss in 1993, he discovered an enterprise, as he put it, 'fat, arrogant, puffed up … inbred and ingrown … dangerously pre-occupied with itself'. Among the first things Gerstner did was scrap the rigid IBM dress code. Big Blue survived – but it was a close call.

6

SNAKES AND LADDERS

So far we have explored the psychological sub-text of the business world in a wide-ranging manner. In one example the number seven plays a prominent part in building a global food empire, in another the chief executive of a hotel chain seeks daily business advice from the Lord during his morning ablutions. The logo of a soap manufacturer is condemned for its alleged diabolical symbolism; a corporate colour is defined through its subconscious associations with male sexuality. An oil company is painted as being in long-term serial denial over its environmental policies; a global automobile brand is judged incapable of remedial action against mounting overseas competition by the very fact of its own past success, a condition attributed to the psychological dynamics of 'the family'. We have heard mention of The Icarus Paradox and Corporate Narcissism.

At the very least, the various examples we have chosen demonstrate the role of myriad unrelated off-balance sheet factors in the evolution of individual companies – from magic numbers and prayer to megalomaniac bosses and the works of Satan. To the lay reader this may suggest a haphazard landscape of corporate psychology that cannot be explained, codified or understood. But that view repeats the common error of mistaking symptom or symbol for cause. H.J. Heinz grew to global status not because of the number seven but because the company's underlying psyche was well attuned to its corporate goals. General Motors ignored the growing threat from Toyota because its psyche had developed a blocked vision derived from many years of unchallenged supremacy in its market. IBM had become 'arrogant and puffed up' by years of market dominance, during which sales were assured by the widespread belief in the technology departments of its customers that 'you never get fired for buying IBM'. The bright red corporate colour of the Virgin

Group suggests a company that has developed a psyche built around a male founder with a strong sexual charge. But what would happen if, at some time in the future, a woman were to take over the helm? Could she reproduce Richard Branson's particular kind of magic? Would this even make sense for the future of the company?

This chapter offers a framework for assessing the 'psychological verities' that characterise different companies and shape their behaviour. One immediate consideration is that every workplace is teeming with discord, power plays and conspiracies. This gets in the way of being able to make perceptual judgements about the business based on what we can call 'truthful reality'. On top of this there may be a history of such 'untruthful' interactions stretching back through many managerial regimes. As a result the company will be left open to errors of judgement and oversight or the equally serious dangers of inaction. Above all, a lack of such truthful reality explains why an organisation fails to achieve awareness or insight about its underlying persona – a failing that may block its capacity to devise successful strategies.

- Why did GM choose to ignore even its own data about the increasing success of emerging Japanese rivals?

- Why did Levi Strauss fail to notice important trends in the global jeans market that threatened its long-term position, or noticed them but refused to act accordingly?

- Why did Body Shop, after many successful years, succumb to skewed perceptions about its market and as a result did not react to major changes in its business sector that threatened its commercial prospects and laid it open to being bought by a global giant?

- Kodak struggled to transform itself from the global symbol of popular photography into an innovatory leader of the digital age – but went adrift in the process. Why?

- Marks & Spencer lost the plot in its clothing business and saw market share plummet, for a while threatening the very survival of the company. Why?

- Digital Equipment Corporation was the world's second biggest computer company in the late 1980s; in 1998 it had become so weak and vulnerable it was gobbled up by Compaq. Why?

In every case failure to achieve awareness or insight at a critical time brought major business problems. But, again, we are only describing the outward manifestations of underlying organisational flaws. As we have made clear, developing a flawed corporate psyche is nothing new; it has been happening as long as corporations themselves have been around. In the old days of producer-driven commerce – where a company could dictate terms to its customers – such failings did not matter. 'Untruthful' companies, with little insight or awareness, could bulldoze their way unchallenged through a marketplace of limited choice, populated by acquiescent consumers and opaque, unregulated business practices. The margin for error was wide enough to protect even the most dysfunctional business from being found out and punished at the checkout.

That protective buffer no longer exists. It has been estimated that over the long average of 20th-century business around 90 per cent of corporate profits were generated by the lack of opportunities available to people for comparing the various products on offer in a particular market. In the very early days of modern business, markets were highly localised, with limited consumer choice – they were seriously imperfect. Even the rise of mass markets in the early post-war years was largely confined to the regional or national space. One could say the most valuable asset on the typical company balance sheet back then was the ignorance of its customers. This ignorance has been steadily transformed by the globalisation of markets and better information flows to a new generation of knowledgeable, demanding and choosy consumers. The age of the Internet, with its comparison engines, online auctions and infinite access to details of products and services, has shifted the rules firmly in favour of the buyer.

Blogging, itself a revolution in the communication of views and verdicts on corporate conduct, product quality and word-of-mouth advice, is rapidly dismantling the firewalls that have long kept consumer knowledge ring-fenced and corporate secrets protected from the public eye. We are on the way to building a near-perfect market for information, and the corporate sector will find itself the most exposed – even more so than government. In this unforgiving, see-through 21st-century business environment any company that hopes to fool itself – and its customers – about its 'truthful reality' will be unpleasantly surprised. Like an individual, a company can con itself and others about its true personality – but not for long. Given time, corporate bullshit may well be one of the great casualties of the World Wide Web.

Clarity the Key

For every company, then, the key to building a healthy psyche lies in addressing the critical issue of 'truthful reality', in developing awareness and insights about the business as a platform for effective decisions and actions. But, as with people, achieving this is easier said than done.

At the core of our analysis is what we call 'perceptual clarity' – the new PC. How clearly does a company understand its true self and use that view of self as the basis for its business approach? With young companies this may include analysing the personality of the company's founder, whenever this is still imprinted on, or intertwined with, the corporate persona. With long-established companies of powerful heritage – Shell, IBM, GE – the focus is instead on the personality traits that have developed and accumulated within the organisation over time beyond individual leaders.

We can explore the various versions of this 'lack of truthfulness' by constructing a ladder of differing psychological states that allows us to assess exactly where an organisation is placed in terms of achieving 'perceptual clarity'. This ladder runs through seven emotions: *inertia, pessimism, timidity, frustration, aggression, arrogance* and *courage*. The lowest three are passive emotions that describe 'frozen' states where nothing goes forward. In common parlance this is about being 'unable to see the wood for the trees'. *Aggression* and *arrogance* are active emotions, though they generate quite different outcomes. *Frustration* is neither: it is best summed up by 'I can see alternatives but I cannot get a grip on a specific line of action.'

But these are not fixed states; there can be movement between the rungs. To take one well-known example, publisher Robert Maxwell, the notorious buyer-and-seller of companies who eventually became the great pension fund plunderer, was more in *arrogance* and *aggression* but went up and down the ladder. People stuck in *timidity* can very easily drop down to *pessimism* and then go up to *frustration*. But they cannot usually move up to *courage*.

Courage is a positive emotion and uniquely so. *Courage* is the highest level of 'perceptual clarity' and the psychological state most readily associated with long-term success. In blunt terms, companies that lack such a level of clarity will constantly underachieve. The higher up the ladder they are, the more likely they are to manage their way through. But unless and until they reach the top, they will never realise their full potential. The lower they are down the ladder, the more likely they will fail. In passing, we make no apology for the fact that our ladder, like the great Heinz corporation and the Book of Revelation, is further evidence of the power of seven in our lives.

COURAGE

ARROGANCE

AGGRESSION

FRUSTRATION

TIMIDITY

PESSIMISM

INERTIA

The Ladder of Perceptual Clarity

The lowest emotional rung, *inertia*, is usually a state of black depression. In people this manifests itself as a total lack of energy; even lifting an arm is difficult. Timid people would be shaking; *inertia* means no movement at all. Their level of clarity is at absolute zero. Everything is black; they cannot discriminate. In a company such a condition invariably comes from a deep-seated belief that the business is not going to make it. It may face bankruptcy or be about to hit rock bottom. Perhaps its shares have taken a nosedive. In the corporate domain, *inertia* is distinguished from other psychological states by a total absence of activity. The UK rail company Railtrack, put into administration by the British government in 2001, could be seen as deeply mired in *inertia* related to a succession of operational and financial disasters, ranging from an unending spate of train crashes to a parlous balance sheet. This resulted in a kind of paralysis that blocked forward progress. One research paper described the company as being 'frozen in the headlights' as it confronted its sorry plight.

Case Study: Fallible Inactivity

The demise of Britain's Railtrack is a powerful example of corporate *inertia* wreaking its destruction. The company was created in 1994 by John Major's Conservative government to run the infrastructure – tracks, signals and stations – used by the country's newly privatised rail franchises. Its flotation on the London Stock Exchange was a hugely over-subscribed success. Many of the company's 250,000 shareholders were small investors hoping to grab a profitable slice of the sell-off of former state-run concerns. In the short run their optimism seemed well judged. From a launch price of 380 pence the shares soared to a high of 1700 pence.

But the euphoria would not last long. To industry watchers Railtrack would soon become synonymous with fallible inactivity, a key reason being that maintenance of the UK rail infrastructure had been handed over to some 2000 subcontractors, who operated under a seemingly haphazard management system. To compound matters, Railtrack had laid off large numbers of staff, even though passenger numbers had risen considerably. According to Chris Green, a former manager with Railtrack's publicly owned predecessor British Rail, 'The net result has been a collective loss of memory on the basics of running a railway.' [1]

Public support for Railtrack steadily declined as Britain's rail network plunged into crisis. Train punctuality deteriorated sharply, damaging the company's reputation with customers and attracting massive fines from rail regulators. Worse still, the network was afflicted by a string of fatal crashes. At the time of the Hatfield crash, Railtrack was alleged to have no clear understanding of the state of the network. Investor confidence evaporated. In October 2001 Railtrack sank into administration and its assets were transferred to Network Rail.

We can diagnose this as a case of the corporate rabbit caught in the headlights – a good example of a company trapped in both *inertia* and probably *timidity*. One could even say that we are looking at a situation where a group of kids have had their train set taken away and they can't play any more. When things started going wrong they were unable to respond – and the rest is history. Contrast the short, disastrous era of Railtrack with, say, the late 1970s when the UK rail system was run by Peter Parker, a great leader and communicator with a clear view of future directions. That is probably the last time Britain's railways were seen in a good light.

Corporate *inertia* can have many causes – perhaps bad luck in a stock market crash, a traumatic shift in market conditions or terrible management that has finally reached the end of its rope. With Railtrack, a highly confusing managerial formula was compounded by what appears to have been a loss of grip on the practicalities of running a railway. Or maybe the leader disappears after many years in the driving seat. One obvious example of this particular version is Marconi – the former General Electric Company. GEC was the creation of Arnold Weinstock, who ran the company for years and built it to greatness. But Weinstock handed his company over to a new management team that seemed to be overtaken by *inertia*. They did not make choices; they could not see choices. Marconi failed abysmally and the brand name no longer exists.

Case Study: Study in Inertia

Britain's Marconi was the former General Electric Company, a corporation built up to world status over four decades by Arnold Weinstock. Its colossal size, backed by an equally huge cash mountain, made GEC an automatic choice for membership of the original *Financial Times* 30-share index. The tide began to turn in 1996 when Weinstock was forced to step down by powerful City institutions that demanded younger management and more aggressive policies. The company's new management staked Marconi's future on a shift away from GEC's traditional core businesses in power generation and heavy engineering into the high-glamour IT and telecoms markets – sectors then enjoying an unprecedented boom in which every commercial decision, it seemed, turned to gold.

But with the turn of the new millennium came the dot-com bust and days of reckoning for over-inflated technology shares. The safety net provided by the legendary billion-pound cash pile inherited from Weinstock had been spent on two expensive US telecoms equipment manufacturers. The Marconi top management team seemed caught like traumatised rabbits in the headlights of commercial Armageddon. The company's reputation, and its share price, went into meltdown. By the time Lord Weinstock died in July 2002 the company was worth less than £150 million. At the height of its power its market capitalisation had stood at £35 billion. In October 2005 the bulk of the business was bought by the Swedish telecoms company Ericsson. What was once the most successful corporation in Britain had disappeared for ever.

The Marconi story is a classic example of corporate *inertia*. The leader has gone and the new leadership soon finds itself in dire straits because of decisions that backfired. Fearful of making further bad decisions and exacerbating things, the company does nothing. At the level of *inertia* an entity does not make choices; it cannot see choices. When seen in individuals, they may have had clinical depression throughout their lives. It is a biochemical condition. Clarity is zero. When this happens to a company it is unlikely to survive. *Inertia* is a 'passive' emotion and passive means nothing gets done. At least *timidity* – further up our PC ladder – means that people are shaking from trepidation or some other variant of fear. With *inertia* there is no shaking at all; there is nothing happening whatsoever.

The critical issue is: can a state of *inertia* be cured? In the cases of Railtrack and Marconi the condition proved terminal: one company collapsed and the other was taken over by a predator. In the realm of human psychology the outcome can go either way. Some people suffer from clinical depression throughout their lives. If this condition were applied to a company, it would not make it. Railtrack and Marconi did not make it.

Alongside the almost moribund mental state of *inertia* are *pessimism* and *timidity*. If clarity is likened to tiny shafts of light, there is no ray of light in *inertia*; it is a kind of stasis. There is a minute amount in *pessimism* and *timidity*. People or organisations displaying these emotional characteristics are not decisive or innovative. When they do take decisions they are likely to be the wrong ones. Where they do possess fragments of clarity, they see no more than a magnified version of their fears. *Pessimism* is about a kind of gloom; bereft, 'griefy' people wallowing in the loss of a loved one are in this state of mind. *Pessimism* would be associated with Marks & Spencer at its lowest and with Swissair, which failed completely. *Timidity* results from a total lack of confidence, an inability to confront anything. It is an expression of an unreasonable level of fear.

These – the lowest three emotions on the ladder – are really about blocked vision: an organisation not being able to see its way ahead. *Frustration*, on the other hand, brings very different problems. It generates unpleasant patterns of behaviour: scheming, cunning, plotting, trying in futile ways. A company locked in *frustration* may have appetite but lacks clarity. Instead it follows a lustful path that seeks to have everything it sees; it risks blundering into all kinds of business adventures without due care and attention to the possible consequences. *Frustration* is a high-risk psychological condition. In the corporate context it helps explain why a company jumps from one venture or market segment to another, with no clear direction. It wants everything, whatever the implications for its psychological balance. At the turn of this new century *frustration* also explains the sad fate of so many dot.com start-ups. Most were eaten up by unsustainable cash-burn rates fuelled by over-ambitious expectations founded on seriously flawed business models. But remember, an organisation sitting in one emotion can move up and down to others. If it is stuck in *timidity*, it can very easily drop down to *pessimism* and then just as easily rise back up to *frustration*.

Let us turn now to the two active emotions. *Aggression* signals a careless 'I am going to have a go no matter what' attitude. It often succeeds temporarily, but bravado and anger are only short-term winners – just as the human emotion of *aggression* is not sustainable for too long. Rupert Murdoch and his News Corporation is the very embodiment of an aggressive corporate psyche at work.

Arrogance, at the top of the ladder of blocking emotions, readily applies to many of the better-known case studies in corporate distress. *Arrogance* is a somewhat delusionary state. It has probably claimed more erstwhile big players than any other emotion. One reason is that an arrogant corporate psyche can very quickly turn to *inertia* and hence court commercial disaster. *Arrogance* in the psychological sense can be likened to a balloon. When it is pricked that inflated sense of importance collapses and you go back to *inertia*. Ironically, there can often be a high level of clarity in an arrogant company, but the condition fosters a complacency that can lead to downfall. *Arrogance* gets in the way of seeing what's going on in the real world.

A company like Levi Strauss, which allowed its global eminence to be eroded by sparky new labels, is testament to the profound dangers of an arrogant corporate outlook. Its marketplace was overtaken by designer madness and affluence-based consumer behaviour. But its core products were needs-driven, not wants-driven. When the market moved on to become one in which customers clamoured for the labels no one else had, the company was caught out of step. It could attempt to address the new competitive threat by aping its competitors, but it would be working at a disadvantage. The decline in the company's fortunes has exacted a heavy price in consumer loyalty: a recent study by consultancy Interbrand identified Levi Strauss as suffering one of the greatest losses in brand value amongst major global companies.

Case Study: Caught with their Pants Down

The rise and fall of great brands always carries instructive lessons for students of corporate mishaps. This particular story is about a humble product that was transformed into a fashion item by the magic wand of popular taste. And then, one day, the magic evaporated.

The Levi Strauss company was to be run by descendants of the original founder for 150 years – until the end of the 20th century. And while the money kept pouring in, these dynastic managers seemed not to recognise the need for dynamic and market-aware business strategies. By the time they did wake up to reality, the damage had been done. The market for blue jeans had moved on. Generations X and Y, younger and choosier successors to the baby boomers, preferred casual wear from newcomers like Gap, Old Navy and Tommy Hilfiger, or high-fashion jeans from smart labels like Gucci. They preferred clothes that matched their own aspirations, not those of their outdated parents' world.

Through the late 1990s Levi Strauss faced an increasingly uphill battle. The company's credit rating sank. From an unassailable global market position 20 years earlier, by 2003 Levi Strauss was confronting the prospect of commercial extinction. Turnover stood at $4 billion; it was the seventh consecutive year of falling sales. In 1996 the figure had been $7 billion. In April 2002 the company announced it was cutting 20 per cent of its workforce. In September 2003 the last remaining factories in the United States and Canada were earmarked for closure.

In December 2003 a desperate Levi Strauss lost its Chief Financial Officer and appointed outside turnaround consultants – a radical departure from a century and a half of cloistered family management. On hearing of the latest woes afflicting Levi Strauss, San Francisco-based fashion industry consultant Harry Bernard commented: 'Hopefully the powers that be overseeing the treatment will see the patient has been getting the wrong drugs.'

Levi Strauss is still a family company, privately owned by descendants of the man who created it. Its website proclaims an unbending sense of moral superiority and brand leadership: 'Levi's jeans are a symbol of freedom and self-expression ... We will clothe the world.' Its business mission reflects four fundamental emotions: 'Empathy – Originality – Integrity – Courage'. Such emotions – as this book makes clear – should ensure its future survival and even a new ascendancy, especially its devotion to *courage*. Somehow we are doubtful.

This is an instructive study in corporate *arrogance*. Instructive because the company actually possessed a high level of clarity but was overtaken by a complacency that in the end produced commercial disaster. *Arrogance* is really extremely vulnerable. From the facts of the case, Levi Strauss thought 'we are it – we are untouchable'. But, rather like Body Shop, it failed to recognise that the marketplace had turned towards designer madness and affluence-driven consumer desires. Today's affluent consumers want uniqueness, but uniqueness is no longer represented by a pair of working pants now worn by millions of everyday people across the world.

The special characteristic that had turned Levi's into a global brand for the post-war baby-boomer generation was its connection with the working-class ethic. Levi pants came from the humble working farmer. Their attraction was in their appeal to everyman – in effect the idea that 'we can all have them'. They sold the same 'whole earth' values typical of that generation. But that has all changed. Consumers now say: 'I want the label no-one else has' or 'I want clothes that reflect my generation'. So companies like Levi Strauss are trapped with product ranges that no longer match new consumer realities.

A somewhat different perspective on *arrogance* applies to Philips, the Dutch electrical company with a well-earned reputation for innovation. Founded in 1891, it helped pioneer the modern consumer electronics age, not least in revolutionary areas like video, and grew to be Europe's biggest electrical enterprise. But they, too, have stumbled in recent years. In the early 1990s, for example, the company burnt its fingers very badly trying to break into the PC market. In the fiercely competitive high-tech market Philips has displayed a serious psychological flaw best described as 'a lack of skills for war'. In terms of our ladder of emotions they are probably in *arrogance* but may already have dropped down to *timidity*. While most companies react appropriately to aggressive competitors, Philips seems to have fallen prey to a mentality that draws on an aversion to conflict: 'We're nice people; we won't fight.' One could almost portray it as Granny dancing at a wedding – trying to be innovative and 'with it', but deep down just an old organisation.

But you don't have to be old to be arrogant. Perhaps the clearest example of misapplying Internet technology to an existing business sector is the California-based start-up Webvan, an online grocery venture set to be one of the darlings of the late-1990s US dot-com boom and a worthy heir to the Silicon Valley inheritance. It turned out to be perhaps the best example of how an arrogant corporate psyche can seriously misread the nature – and future – of the online revolution and lead investors to bet the farm and more on a doomed business idea.

This now-defunct company exemplified all the worst attributes of the dot-com frenzy: poor strategic thinking, excessive exuberance and lavish spending. In both its business model and its behaviour Webvan was trapped in a psychological demeanour that guaranteed early failure. The company's founders made the classic mistake of wanting to re-invent an industry – in this case food shopping – that was not ready for it and maybe never would be. They couldn't even break into it as uninvited guests: going to market with a totally unknown brand name meant they had to spend 30 per cent of sales on marketing, a catastrophic formula in an already cash-strapped enterprise.

Commentators said online groceries was at best a niche market but with no history could not be analysed sufficiently to support a feasible business plan. Webvan begged to differ and its backers paid a huge price.

Case Study: Food and Sex are Special

This optimistic start-up, based in Foster City, California went public in 1999 and nailed its corporate colours – and over a billion in venture capital dollars – to the dot-com mast in the rock-solid belief that 'the future of shopping was online'. Neighbourhood grocery stores were out, said Webvan; people would vote with their plastic in favour of buying eggs, butter and deli items over the Internet. Customers were offered delivery within a 30-minute window of their choosing. Time-pressed middle-class Americans, Webvan promised, would take to it like the Internet itself.

For a while it seemed the bright young things at Webvan had called it right. The shares rocketed to a high of $30. Investors saw their initial funding of $375 million translated into a corporate worth of $1.2 billion. A euphoric Webvan management signed up contracting giant Bechtel for a $1 billion deal to build a string of $30 million high-tech warehouses spanning the nation. Pretty soon the company was trading in seven major US cities and the future was rocking.

But Webvan's precocious success was a delusion – and short lived. The 'future of shopping' was not yet ready to comply with the company's vision. Customers stayed away; in those early years of Net-based commerce fewer than 2 per cent of Americans switched to on-line shopping and then only faint-heartedly. Webvan sales stagnated while their cash burn accelerated, quickly gobbling up more than a billion dollars. Its shares fell to just 6 cents. In July 2001 Webvan filed for bankruptcy. Some 2000 employees lost their jobs. Meanwhile, a lawsuit was filed against senior officers of the company alleging that its prospectus to investors contained 'materially false and misleading information'. Whatever the outcome, this Icarus-like venture had crashed and burned. A sarcastic senior Gartner analyst commented: 'Here is a radical thought – the future of the online grocer market belongs to the grocery stores. They know the business.'

Where did Webvan go wrong? First, the venture's ambitious founders were determined to emulate Jeff Bezos, the creator of

Amazon. But there were critical differences between the two business ideas. Above all, books are not food, with all that implies for storage and handling. Books are also easier to deliver – you cannot post butter or beefsteak through a letter box. In addition, research shows that Amazon customers are less angry at delays compared to someone awaiting tubs of ice cream or fresh fruit salad. The best route for Webvan would have been partnering with existing supermarket chains to piggyback on their expertise and facilities. Britain's supermarket giant Tesco has become one of the world's most successful online grocers by bolting its online division onto an existing network of stores and warehouses and leveraging its strong brand among current and potential customers. Tesco asked its customers how they wanted things and encouraged them to continue shopping in the traditional way. Instead of building fancy warehouses, it kept the 'shop' at the centre of the offer, with customer orders picked from nearby supermarkets before delivery. Another UK online grocery venture, Ocado (run by high-street retailer Waitrose) follows a similar path. Webvan never considered this option: not a single member of its top management team or investor group had any management experience in the supermarket industry. They hired their chief executive from Andersen Consulting.

Second, Webvan seemed gripped by the kind of grandiosity of mind seen with Enron at its worst. Millions were spent on fleets of smart delivery trucks and a vast array of high-tech toys to drive its online ambitions, including 30 massive Sun Microsystems servers and all the trimmings. More was wasted on office furnishings, including hordes of $800 chairs. The company was equally generous with its compensation packages, attracting criticism around the markets for agreeing a severance package for CEO George Shaheen of $375,000 a year – for the rest of his life.

Here again we are probably looking at *arrogance*. No doubt their research told them consumers were changing but they did not bring a wider range of values into their business thinking. You have to be very careful about anything to do with food for sustenance. It is a primary survival affinity – sex and food are the basic human drives. When you are considering primary survival instincts like procreation and food you cannot move beyond the intangibles. People want to smell, touch and see their food before buying it. Procreation also presupposes sensory involvement. You can, of course, have pornography on the internet, but this will not produce children – it is not about survival. Some grocery retailers – like Tesco and Ocado – have devised a successful online formula based around traditional stores. Webvan set out to revolutionise a sector rooted in old-fashioned emotional connections with food and refused to accept that most people prefer traditional ways of buying their groceries.

The mistake Webvan made was that it believed technology could change people's behaviour in this vital area. Essentially, the business premise created isolation. For some areas of online retailing this isolation is not an issue. But, contrary to Webvan's operating principle, people like the social aspects of shopping rather than sitting in front of a computer – certainly where food is concerned and even for clothing. Its business vision was not totally incorrect; where it went wrong was in seriously overestimating how quickly consumers would embrace the concept. To achieve Webvan's much-vaunted 30-minute delivery offer called for a huge investment in logistics infrastructure, which in turn generated high-pressure investor demand for speedy returns through rapidly growing sales. But the sales just did not come quickly enough. The company it sought to emulate, Amazon, avoided this trap; it invested lightly at start-up, building infrastructure as revenues and business growth allowed.

Arrogance has claimed many corporate victims over the years. It also explains, for example, why the Lloyd's of London insurance market convinced itself (erroneously) in the late 1980s and early 1990s that nothing could touch it. Lloyd's only survived after much pain, many individual bankruptcies and a radical overhaul. More recently scandal-ridden corporations like Enron, WorldCom, Parmalat and others fell prey to the same destructive emotional state. On the other hand, Enron's auditors, Arthur Andersen, who sank with the Enron ship, would be most closely linked to a mixture of *frustration* and *arrogance*.

The highest emotion on the ladder is *courage*. It is also the only positive emotion in our ranking of seven and the one most closely identified with sustainable business success. *Courage* is about having clarity – about knowing what you want and going straight for it. Clarity can be described as 'appropriate awareness or insight'. If a company fails to ask tough questions about itself and remains ignorant about its true personality – lacking clarity or insight – it may accidentally succeed. But in the long run that organisation and its people will find themselves trapped in inappropriate behaviours. And failure may not be far behind.

Case Study: Jack The Ripper – Clarity Works

Perhaps the most successful corporate boss in history took US conglomerate General Electric to pole position in 20 years of tough, uncompromising leadership renowned for a hatred of unclear thinking. Jack Welch, the son of a railroad conductor, worked his way through college to attain a PhD in 1960. His first – and only – job was with GE, which he joined that same year. His rise through the ranks of GE management was meteoric. In 1981 he became the company's youngest-ever CEO.

He immediately set about a programme of radical transformation, stripping out the 'old guard' of top executives and dismantling the company's bureaucracy. He believed in routinely eliminating the lowest-performing 10 per cent of management, a habit that earned him the nickname 'Neutron Jack', a reference to a Cold War nuclear weapon concept designed to take out people without damaging the buildings. During his tenure more than 100,000 jobs disappeared. Welch had a noted aversion for what he called 'superficial congeniality' – a category of bullshit – and transgressors were treated summarily.

His aim was to re-invent GE to make it fit for the 21st century. The company was moved out of manufacturing and into services. From a business founded in 1878 as the Edison Electric Light Company, Welch turned GE into a fit-for-the-future leading-edge enterprise spread across diversified technology, media and financial services.

His transformational magic performed miracles for the GE balance sheet. When Jack Welch took over as CEO the company's annual revenues stood at $26.8 billion; when he retired they had grown to $130 billion. Under his leadership GE shares went up 4000 per cent. In 2004 GE was valued at $400 billion, which made it the world's number-one corporation in terms of market capitalisation.

In 1999 Jack Welch was named 'Manager of the Century' by *Fortune* magazine. A few years later, in an interview with a British newspaper, he summed up his management philosophy: 'I want bosses to have more candour, less bullshit'.[2]

Jack Welch had a reputation as an excessively hard-headed, unsentimental hire-and-fire merchant. Yet it seems like a very good example of high levels of 'perceptual clarity' and *courage* at work. *Courage* does not have to be nice, only clear. It is not about an unkind person, simply one who is firm, calm, confident. *Courage* is like a silver sword; it does not bleed. It cuts through bullshit. In a company, clarity is about knowing what your aims are and getting on with achieving them. There is incredible vision and focus. A courageous business leader sticks with what he or she knows. But this should not be confused with a bullying personality, which is based on anger and *aggression*, an emotion that blocks everything. Or if a CEO is in *arrogance*, that person may be pretending to be someone else – what Welch himself refers to as 'superficial congeniality', offering a misleading face to others. And that can never be good for the health of the business. It's not easy to achieve *courage* – you have to be very integrated as a person. Welch seems to have possessed such qualities.

In people *courage* is unique because it does not to have to rely on the failings of others. It is not about being smug and proud; *courage* is a very humble emotion. In contrast, an emotion like *arrogance* needs other people in order to exist. By patronising others an arrogant person gains feelings of superiority and well-being. Being in *courage* means that you do not wish others to be lower than you; on the contrary, you want others to rise up to your level. *Courage* means I have no need either to control you or to seek your approval. It also means I will not allow you to control me. You can define it as a kind of contained personality. Anyone else with the same level of confidence will enjoy hanging out with you. There is no battle of egos confusing or complicating matters. It is an empowered and therefore an empowering state. In the corporate arena, *courage* expresses itself through an ethos of clarity about business goals and the means to achieve them. It is not sentimental; the organisation has an objective and there are no other negative emotions getting in the way.

At times one can also speak of selective *courage*, with this emotion acting within the company but not in an individual's personal sphere outside it. Some might say that a highly successful and widely admired business leader like the CEO of BP, John Browne – now Lord Browne – who has only ever worked for that company since leaving university, invested most of his personal emotional capital in the success of the enterprise. Colleagues say he married the business; under his management it grew to be the world's largest oil company in terms of revenues and second only to Wal-Mart in the corporate revenue rankings.[3] In his working style he seems to display all the characteristics of *courage*, being very much his own man, with an uncluttered view. He admits to a dislike of management texts, preferring instead to read books on Venice. He has developed his own philosophy about business success, with the help of visionaries like Intel's Andy Grove. Browne's formula comes across as clear and simple, with no Machiavellian sub-text: 'It needs to be based on a rational, logical and carefully thought-through structure. It's about leadership and motivation and energising people … the most important thing is never to lose the plot.'[4] But on another plane it is possible to see Lord Browne's self-evident lifetime devotion to the success of BP as a displacement for not being quite as 'courageous' in his own life.

Whatever the personal dimension, a courageous company knows the truth about itself and frames its plans accordingly. It is not afraid to speak its mind. It builds its strategies and serves its customers on the basis of total honesty about itself – its beliefs, aims and ways of doing business.

The bullshit factor is zero. In the 21st-century marketplace courageous companies will be a breed apart – the winning breed. Two UK companies that come to mind as presenting a high level of 'perceptual clarity' are Churchill Insurance and the innovative soap retailer Lush, now operating close to 200 outlets in more than two dozen countries. Both are fairly recent start-ups. Both were built on a very clear and simple vision of their business purpose. Both are very successful. Churchill's founder Martin Long actually put the word 'courage' at the heart of its corporate mission statement, while the company's 'keep-it-simple' approach to customer communications has earned it the Crystal Mark for linguistic clarity from the Plain English Campaign. Lush, founded by Mark Constantine, ploughs the furrow Webvan decided to ignore – our sensory relationship with shopping – and sells soap as if it were food, encouraging customers to smell and touch products on display in a deli setting.

Many examples of corporate *courage* seem to be seen where the founder-leader is still running the business. Michael Dell of Dell Computers seems a good candidate, with a highly specific sense of business purpose and an equally clear vision of what the business is not about. Another is Stelios Haji-Ioannou, the Greek-born entrepreneur who launched the UK-based no-frills airline easyJet in 1995 and built it into a billion-dollar group embracing Internet cafés, financial services, car rental, cinemas, hotels, pizza delivery, buses and a steadily expanding range of other businesses founded on a central principle of low-cost, no-nonsense, value-for-money offers to the customer. Stelios believes you must tell it how it is. When you log off in one of his Internet cafés you see a message that says: 'Please take your rubbish with you – your mother doesn't work here.' It is signed 'Stelios'. He is no fan of corporate bullshit.

Business history suggests that senior companies with many generations of heritage find it extremely difficult to maintain the clarity that seems essential for sustained success. Their corporate state of mind carries the accumulated baggage of past actions, wrong and right. Deep-rooted ideas and experiences weigh like religious beliefs on their decision-making. Either they re-invent themselves and rediscover *courage* or they face an unpromising future and may fall by the wayside. As observed earlier, the average lifespan of a *Fortune 500* company is about 30 years – the equivalent of the lifetime of a primitive hunter-gatherer several millennia ago. Looked at this way, modern corporations are still an endangered species and the major contributory factor in their high mortality rate is a blocked forward vision caused by delusional, arrogant or complacent thinking. *Courage* is very rare; there are not many courageous people and the same applies to companies.

Part Three

A WINNING FORMULA

7

THREE FACES OF COURAGE

The central theme of *The Bullshit Factor* is that organisations and people inhabit the same psychological universe and that, like people, organisations can have psychological issues. These issues are manifested in patterns of behaviour that reflect levels of 'untruthfulness', misperceptions, delusions or some other deceit. Examples of such behavioural manifestations have been examined in some detail in earlier sections of this book. Chapter 6 spells out the various emotional states that can produce the phenomenon of the 'psychotic company' – an organisation afflicted, in one form or another, by an emotional state that leads to blocked vision – and explains why such a company is unlikely to survive and prosper in the long term. In our case studies we examine companies that have suffered serious commercial consequences, even terminal decline, because of certain psychotic traits that were left uncorrected.

But we also focus on the idea of the 'courageous company', one possessing a high degree of 'perceptual clarity' that enables it to develop an uncluttered vision of its business purpose and future strategy. Such a company has significant potential for success in the years ahead. As earlier chapters have demonstrated, few organisations achieve such a level of 'perceptual clarity' and *courage* and, as a result, are always at risk. The ever-growing list of corporate failures is, indeed, a catalogue of companies that suffered the consequences of a dysfunctional psyche, with or without dishonest intent. For every Enron or Parmalat, where criminal wrong-doing led to collapse, there is another leading business name that innocently disappeared from view for the simple reason that its blocked vision prevented the changes necessary for it to react to new competitive challenges. Meanwhile, many companies still doing perfectly legal business today are afflicted by some psychological malaise and may not be long for this world.

So what lessons can we draw from their plight? What are the key characteristics of this 'courageous company'? How can these characteristics be acquired? Is there such a thing as a winning formula that can promote a healthy corporate psyche and lay the foundations for a successful business?

This challenge has three dimensions. All of them concern people: consumers, employees and business leaders. In all three cases it is vital to develop a sound psychological environment. In turn this will promote sound behaviours and bullshit-free corporate trappings, whether these be logos, liveries, headquarters, language or marketing promises. The courageous company must have an honest and transparent relationship with its customers and a clear understanding of their wants. It must have a mix of employees that matches the psychological demands of the business it is in and the goals it wants to achieve. It must have a top management team that possesses the qualities of integrity and authenticity needed to build a courageous enterprise. And this spirit of integrity must embrace everybody in the organisation, from junior to most senior. Only then can it hope to foster a corporate personality with a vision that is not blocked by dysfunctional emotional baggage.

The Post-Freudian Consumer

It is, of course, a truism to say that a company exists because of its customers. But the idea of 'the customer' has changed considerably over the years. Earlier pages have made reference to the emerging phenomenon of what some call the 'emotional marketplace'. Unfortunately for them, many companies have failed to make the necessary changes and have fallen out of step with the people without whom they cannot survive. Until now these companies have deluded themselves about the new realities of consumer behaviour and about their own preparedness, but such an outlook cannot work for ever. A key task for every organisation is to have an informed appreciation of the fundamental shift in the customer equation over recent years and to apply its lessons to their business thinking.

Here again we see a three-phase pattern of evolution. In the 1900s, markets were still localised and unstructured, but retailers like Sears in the United States and Sainsbury's in the United Kingdom were beginning to aggregate demand and standardise supply with the support of major consumer goods producers like Procter & Gamble and Lever Brothers (later Unilever). Production and distribution costs fell steadily and product innovation accelerated. By the 1950s, mass markets had developed to a point where they could be segmented into sub-markets and targeted by marketing and advertising strategies. The various segments were defined not only by demographic characteristics (which help identify *who* might buy your product) but also by psychographics – the science of working out *why* particular groups of people *want* to buy from you. Marketing campaigns were devised so as to differentiate a product from any competitors and to fit specific segments. Both those earlier mass markets and the later segmented – but still very large – sub-markets are rightly referred to as 'mass markets'.

Crucially, corporate structures and management practices evolved to reflect this mass-market ethos, as did the underlying psyche of the organisation. And this is where the seeds of later problems were sown. Many business organisations became psychological prisoners of a mass-market mentality and were to make very heavy weather of managing the transition to a third phase, one characterised by the totally different customer environment that began to emerge as the century edged towards its close. Some have already perished in the process and others will no doubt follow them in years to come unless they radically transform themselves.

What these companies failed to keep pace with was a total revolution in buying habits – a step-change in the sociology of consumption. Harvard Business School author Jonathan Byrnes captures the essence of this revolution in 'The Age of Precision Markets', published by the School in April 2005:[1]'We are entering a new era in business. The changes we are beginning to experience are as profound and disruptive as those that occurred when roads were first paved, local markets began to join together and mass markets first developed.' The new era Byrnes refers to is defined by a new relationship between producers and consumers based on customised product offers precisely tailored to individual wants. This is very different from a mass-market approach, where a manufacturer develops and produces goods and then sells them to a broad, homogeneous customer base. In the early years of mass markets the manufacturer might not even consult its customers about what they wanted; they were assumed to be grateful for the opportunity to buy. In contrast, a precision marketer will identify a narrow front of selling opportunity – a specific group of consumers that fit a certain profile – and make the deepest possible incursion into this niche marketplace.

A good example of this shift to precision markets is the business model developed by Michael Dell. Instead of designing and building computing equipment and then going out in search of customers, Dell Computers does the reverse: it carefully selects its customers and then individualises every transaction, changing product features and pricing as necessary to clinch the deal – and please the customer. This is not only a break with the mass-market tradition, it also calls for a different kind of company. Mass-market organisations developed 'silos' of management, strictly separated one from the other and each with a different function. During the mass-market years the marketing silo came to enjoy special influence. The pyramid-shaped organisational charts introduced by David McCallum in the mid-19th century, which became so beloved of management gurus, are the visual manifestation of the silo company. But this no longer suits the very different conditions of the new consumer marketplace. As Byrnes puts it: 'Precision markets offer a new way of thinking about a business ... developing these markets requires an organic, whole-business response that goes far beyond classical marketing.'

At the same time, consumers are changing in a way that confronts mass-market companies with a massive challenge. How do we reach this new consumer? How and where do we engage them? People are no longer interested in commodity products and services or the mass-marketing techniques used to convince them to buy. Today's customer wants to feel pampered and unique, making purchases that are relevant and 'authentic', or even frivolous and fun. Old-style consumers were couch potatoes, passively absorbing advertising messages. New consumers want to take control of media content and shape it to their personal interests. Old consumers sought to keep up with the crowd; the new want to stand out from it. The old were served by a small group of information channels; the new have hundreds, from online connections, mobile phones, PDAs and other devices to proliferating, interactive broadcast programming. Instead of big brands, new consumers want niche products that are closely relevant to their individual lifestyle needs and send out signals about personal choices and values. Not for nothing is it referred to as the 'Who-Am-I?' marketplace.

This well-informed, aspirational 21st-century consumer is not easily fooled. Yet despite this, most advertising and marketing strategies still rely heavily on what the psychologist might call 'post-Freudian techniques for reaching and influencing the subliminal'. This approach came to dominate selling practices in the years of growing mass markets after the Second World War. Business became very good at inventing needs, then providing for those needs, then inventing related needs and so on. Traditional marketing techniques exploited the neurotic and dysfunctional parts of consumer identity instead of enhancing the healthy non-neurotic aspects. The psychological dynamics often used in marketing and sales campaigns targeted delusional and addictive processes that are latent but easily encouraged in most human personalities. This emphasis on using psychological levers to manipulate the consumer in turn reflects a dishonest and manipulative psyche within the organisation itself. Beware: a company that relies on delusional marketing tactics increasingly deludes itself. More importantly, other businesses also get wise and in their turn exploit the arrogance of the erstwhile market leader and replace it with their own brand of delusions. But the consumer also gets wise to it sooner or later – and in many product areas that time has all but arrived.

As a result of new consumer attitudes and the shift to what Byrnes has called 'precision marketing', mass market 'delusional' methods are past their sell-by date and – for those companies still relying on them – simply reflect outmoded and possibly dysfunctional traits that could be deeply damaging to the long-term prospects of the business. Indeed, it is a sign of the desperation that has engulfed some in the marketing world that they now try to shift product by resorting to the ultimate in surreptitious psychological games – 'stealth marketing'. In the words of an article in *The California Management Review*: 'Stealth marketing attempts to catch people at their most vulnerable by identifying the weak spot in their defensive shields'.[2] It is difficult to imagine a more bullshit-ridden approach to persuading customers to buy.

The main objective of stealth marketing is to persuade the right people to think and talk favourably about a product without letting on that the exercise is company-sponsored. Put another way, it is about conning consumers into liking your product by using a highly distorted version of 'reality'. Thus, actors might be despatched to use a product visibly and convincingly in a place where target consumers are known to congregate, or perhaps talk up the product to people they meet. A Japanese company is said to have paid actors to pose as 'tourists' visiting Staten Island, handing their smart new phone-cameras to passers-by to take pictures of them. In this way, people 'accidentally discovered' the easy-to-use properties and other gee-whiz benefits of the company's latest product offering. A US soft drinks company has enlisted teenage bloggers to hype a new milk product online, pretending to be an authentic voice from the streets. The risks associated with discovery, however, are colossal. Nobody likes to be treated like an idiot.

So an absolutely crucial factor in developing a winning formula is the company's perception of the personality of the consumer in this changing marketplace. Is the business truly keeping up with what people want to buy – and why they want to? If the psyche of the company is too arrogant (and therefore resistant to adapting to changing consumer realities), the consumer's intelligence often gets ignored in the delusion-driven language of an over-sophisticated marketing strategy built on manipulative research. And if the company is still trapped in a mass-market mentality, the chances of escaping from this arrogant state are even more remote. It is a somewhat sad side-effect of our consumer society that its basic human dynamic is dysfunctional – addictive and stuck in *frustration*.

A Free Agent Future

The second dimension of our winning formula is the make-up of a company's employees. Understanding the dreams and desires of its customers is of no use if the people who actually run the business are singing from a different song sheet. What mix of talents and outlook will best underwrite its chances of success in the future?

For several reasons this issue is becoming increasingly complicated as the nature of working structures shifts. Technologies are driving profound changes in the operational characteristics of the enterprise. The virtual possibilities of the future 'connected' economy means companies are breaking free of long-standing practices of fixed workplace location, centralised management and 9-to-5 schedules. Many functions traditionally performed within a corporate structure are moving outside. Important support functions will be entrusted to external contractors; outsourcing and off-shoring are nothing new and these practices will grow further in the years ahead. Other roles in the traditional workforce are being taken over by 'contingent' employees, hired as and when needed. Meanwhile, growing demands for a better balance between work pressures and personal life are pushing in a similar direction.

Many business sectors will see the emergence of 'virtual corporations', eco-systems of different specialisms brought together to handle specific projects and then released back into the skills market to serve other needs. In the US economy millions of adult workers now describe themselves as 'free agents' – specialists and consultants who work for a portfolio of employers. Some 45 million Americans are now classified as 'teleworkers' who do not make the daily commute to some corporate HQ or related facility. Instead, they work in homes, cars, satellite offices or other premises remote from the company they service. In Europe estimates of the total teleworker population range from 25 to 30 million and it is growing fast.

Such trends reflect the evolving nature of 'the company' and its workforce relationships. In the archetype version of tomorrow's company the permanent core of management will decrease in size and its shape will move from the 'pyramid/hierarchy' of the old industrial enterprise towards a more amorphous amoeba-like form that mutates to accommodate current needs of the business. The headquarters function will steadily diminish and eventually could even disappear. More people will work outside the company than within it. But this does not dispense with the core challenge of making sure that your 'team' – internal and external – has a psychological disposition that matches and reinforces the company's aims for the time it is collectively pursuing the same goal. Quite the contrary, it merely makes it far more difficult.

But, in essence, the challenge remains the same. If a business is to succeed in achieving its chosen goals, it is essential to recruit and build a team of people whose psychological demeanour matches the persona of the company for whom they will work and the goals it has set itself. The honest truth is that when it comes to hiring staff, there is no such thing as one-size-fits-all. Round pegs do not, as a rule, work well in square holes, no matter how much retraining is thrown at them. A mindset that may be right for a design company is almost certainly not suitable for a law firm or merchant bank. The best people for a construction firm are unlikely to suit a healthcare business, far less a magazine publisher or fashion house. This applies even within the various parts of a company: different departments need different types of people according to the job they do. An advertising agency's creative team, for example, calls for a psychological profile quite distinct from that needed, say, by someone working in its payroll or accounts department or managing its corporate vehicle fleet.

But this is a two-way street. Employees considering a move to another job should also think about whether they match up with the company they may be about to join. Do its aspirations mirror your own? Do you have an appropriate communication style and abilities? Why did you choose to work there in the first place? Will you be able to attain your best potential and will your potential promote the business? If an individual makes the wrong choice, the company suffers. If the company deceives that individual, both suffer. But if both have got it right, both benefit. It is not enough to have the right academic qualifications; we must also consider people skills and emotional intelligence. The workplace is a cauldron of dynamics – microcosms of the many worlds we inhabit. As we have pointed out earlier, in some key respects business organisations are akin to family structures that teem with discord and ambition. They can be a minefield of psychological conflicts.

A critical element of building a healthy corporate psyche is the trade-off between creativity and IQ within its talent pool. In the context of working abilities there are four basic personality types and they can be represented by a symbol:

- Higher IQ / Higher Creativity   SPIRAL
- Higher IQ / Lower Creativity   CUBE
- Lower IQ / Lower Creativity   SQUARE
- Lower IQ /Higher Creativity   SQUIGGLE

This range of personalities can be expressed as a four-box chart similar to that of a traditional SWOT analysis of strengths, weakness, opportunities and threats. The two axes are Creativity Low–High and IQ Low–High. The chart can be used to plot where a company's talent mix should ideally be located and as a diagnostic tool to identify where a company may be unbalanced in how it recruits its staff.

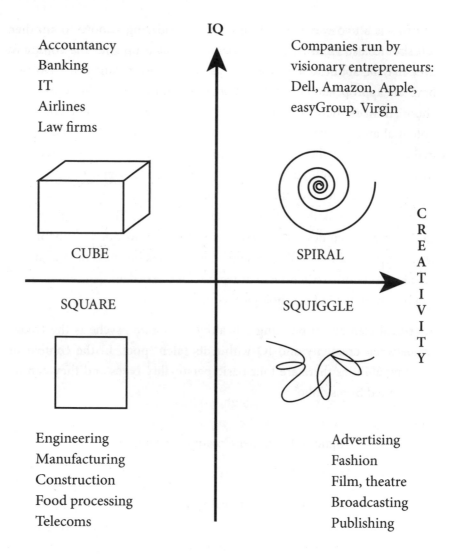

IQ

Accountancy
Banking
IT
Airlines
Law firms

Companies run by
visionary entrepreneurs:
Dell, Amazon, Apple,
easyGroup, Virgin

CUBE

SPIRAL

CREATIVITY

SQUARE

SQUIGGLE

Engineering
Manufacturing
Construction
Food processing
Telecoms

Advertising
Fashion
Film, theatre
Broadcasting
Publishing

Talent Mix: IQ + EQ

If the combination of personality types within a company is wrongly
matched to its business profile, it will not operate successfully for
long. A bank, for example, needs more *cubes*, people high in IQ
but not necessarily highly creative. An advertising agency or media
company must have *squiggles*, people with strength in high creativity.
Manufacturing companies can succeed even without either of these

attributes, but they do need the low-IQ, low-creative solidity of *squares*. This also applies to differing functions within a company. The finance or treasury department, for instance, can work well if staffed by *cubes* but will need a very different talent mix from, say, a marketing department heavily reliant on *squiggles*.

There is no formula that is perfect for all: success depends on having a people mix that matches the specific needs of the company in its chosen marketplace to its generic profile. For instance, many dot-com start-ups that have succeeded were led by *spirals* – visionary entrepreneurs with a large appetite for risk. Amazon.com and its founder-leader Jeff Bezos is the obvious example. A more recently arrived entrepreneur like Stelios Haji-Ioannou, the easyJet founder, is also a visionary *spiral* and a somewhat special case. He straddles both conventional business and the dot-com sector by attacking mature conventional markets – airlines, car rental, finance, cinemas, hotels, pizzas – with a very strong web-based strategy backed by a simple, clearly-articulated business model.

Most of the people who became dot-com failures were *squiggles*. They failed either because they were high risk-taking, creative types who were nevertheless very bad team-players or were highly creative and energised but lacked the experience to develop a sound business model. On the other hand, the problems at Marks & Spencer, a UK retail brand with a heritage stretching back to 1894, were rooted in serious shortcomings in its clothing/fashion activities. The tribulations of M&S as it attempted to reverse a sales slump that set in during the late 1990s exemplify the dangers of appointing a *cube* to head up a fashion business. A succession of changes to the company's top team arrested the decline but has left many business analysts with a view that M&S has lost its traditional assurance – its clarity.

No More Nightmares?

So the talent mix of a company must reflect its personality as an organisation and what it wants to achieve and present no obstacles to achieving those goals. This will differ from business to business and sector to sector. The challenge is partly an *intellectual* process: 'What is our goal and what is in our way?' But though the answers are produced intellectually, they must be matched by the right *emotional* state of mind. An organisation's intelligence must be connected to its emotional clarity. Putting it in crude algebraic terms: Corporate Success = IQ + EQ.

In other words, the two have to be integrated to create a truly courageous corporate mindset. As with individuals, an organisation must be in touch with what its intellect is doing emotionally. If its emotional intelligence lacks clarity, there will be problems. Like a learned professor, we can be intellectually clever but also emotionally autistic. In a company the IQ elements can be fully in place; the corporate vision can be persuasively enshrined in bullet points and planning charts. To the outside eye it can look dynamic, purposeful and set for greatness. But if the EQ elements – how employees are treated, how corporate goals are discussed and agreed, how ethical issues are addressed – are not in harmony, then the corporate psyche is out of balance and trouble could lie ahead.

This harmony can only be achieved if the third of our triptych of *courage*, the company's leadership team, have the right psychological qualities to meet the challenge. And here, too, there is a considerable mountain to climb. We are talking about nothing less than a revolution in how senior managers view their role and the purpose of the company they run. One driver of this revolution is the collapse of confidence in business leadership triggered by the dishonesty pandemic, discussed in Chapter 4, that has graced myriad media headlines in recent years.

The reaction in the United States was as harsh as anywhere and was summed up comprehensively by Kurt Eichenwald in the *New York Times* in October 2002.[3] After a summer punctuated by successive trials of white-collar defendants accused of corporate crimes he wrote: 'In truth, executives have reached a turning point in terms of their relationship with the public and their place in American society. For decades they have been revered, granted near-superstar status as they dangled the prospect of an ever-improving economy and growing stock portfolios. Now they are the stuff of ridicule, literally portrayed in the Sunday comics as the monsters of children's nightmares.'

This reverence for business superstars stretched to the very top of government; pampering the corporations became a matter of political policy. During the height of the pro-business era of US President Ronald Reagan, 50 of the biggest US corporations avoided paying any federal income tax. By historical analogy, modern corporations had inherited the power and privileges of the aristocracy of the *Ancien Régime* before the French Revolution. During the cataclysm of 1789 popular fury was directed at the bloated and uncaring religious corporations of the Catholic Church. This fury was so great that mobs tore down France's biggest monastery, the Abbey at Cluny, and the Benedictine Order it symbolised was suppressed. Some have mused how this might be a portent of the fate awaiting today's corporations unless they tend to the deepening crisis afflicting their public reputation.

Others point to the collapse in behavioural standards that has accompanied the burgeoning power and privileges of corporate boardrooms and the relentless pressure on them to produce record-beating earnings and a rising share price. Arthur P. Brief, Professor of Business Ethics at Tulane University, puts it thus: 'We have infused so much money and power in executives that they have started to behave as if they are above the rules that govern the rest of us.'[4] In defence of many of these executives, they invariably started out as solid citizens. In the words of Professor Sandra Waddock, of the Carroll School of Management: 'Most people who have fallen victim to the logic of shareholder-only performance that creates the context for wrongdoing are probably decent people led astray by lack of self-examination and moral compass.'[5]

Perhaps the most telling comment on this decline in corporate credibility came from John Brennan, Chairman of Vanguard, a huge US mutual fund group managing investments worth $750 billion. Alarmed by the crumbling of corporate truthfulness, Vanguard – whose Pledge to

Clients centres on a 'plain talk philosophy' – wrote to some 450 public corporations setting out a checklist of proper conduct it expected from companies whose shares it held. Brennan focused on the virus of corporate bullshit: 'It is absolutely clear that the mantra of growth at all costs, and the lionised CEO who could spin a great story, is gone.'[6]

In place of spin, there has to be a new agenda for corporate leaders. They have to shed the legacy of the mighty industrial corporations that sought to carry all before them. Some progress has been made in this regard, but the shadow of Henry Ford and his like still falls across the landscape of management. Too many business leaders across the world still want only to 'win', no matter what the cost to others. They have to escape from the role they have taken upon themselves as blinkered 'instruments of the corporation'. In grand terms, we need a *metanoia* – a shift of mind – in how business decision-makers see themselves, their companies and their markets. This does not mean adopting codes of behaviour that conflict with sound business management. On the contrary, conduct driven by a healthy corporate psyche is the surest foundation for financial success: an organisation that denies its social responsibilities, holds false perceptions about itself, shelters behind delusions or develops an unhealthy relationship with the truth will, eventually, hit trouble. Our corporate culture has to rediscover the values of 'self-examination and moral compass' and place them at the heart of the business.

The courageous company needs to deploy not just silver-sword clarity and a truthful outlook but also integrity and principled leadership. Trust and fairness are guiding traits. And all spring from sound psychological roots. It is worth noting that 'integrity' means 'wholeness' or 'completeness' – the foundations of a healthy psyche. But the awkward thing about such qualities is that they cannot be created by rules, regulations and codes of ethics. They have to be inherent in the individual. Psychologist Lawrence Kohlberg, for instance, maintains that people (and therefore companies) who need to be cajoled into good behaviour with threats of regulatory or other legal sanctions are at the lowest level of moral development, just like a persistently naughty child who can only be kept in check through ever-present threats of punishment.

Kohlberg, a Harvard professor, shared Harry Frankfurt's keen interest in morality and behaviour. He developed a six-stage classification of how people progress their moral reasoning, arranged over three ascending levels. The first two levels are acquired during childhood and then adult life and embrace basic moral principles sufficient to get by in society without ending up in jail. The third level is more elevated and relates to an understanding of social mutuality and a genuine interest in the welfare of others, manifested in respect for the 'social contract' and a principled conscience – precisely the qualities missing in the avaricious, mendacious, asocial corporations that have fed the scandal frenzy of recent years.

Ominously, Kohlberg concluded from his studies that only a tiny percentage of adults ever attain this third level. Taking our premise of 'the corporation as a psychological entity', it seems reasonable to argue that very few companies will develop the 'principled conscience' vital to creating a bullshit-free business environment. But the argument runs deeper. This culture of principles is not only about the characteristics of leadership: the entire organisation needs to be on board. Courageous leaders may set the tone, but employees must be involved in the process of courage-building, ideally taking ownership of it. And this takes us full circle, back to the process by which companies choose their employee teams.

This 'virtuous circle' is the subject of a report called *Integrity in Practice*, commissioned by Britain's Financial Services Authority and published in 2003.[7] Co-author Roger Steare, an 'occupational philosopher' and specialist in workplace ethics, has spent his career studying the moral dimensions of the working environment. His conclusions are highly relevant to the challenge of bringing the courageous qualities of clarity, honesty and integrity into the corporate psyche. They describe a belief system in which people make a clear distinction between the standards of behaviour they apply in their personal lives and those they follow when in 'company' mode:

- When people arrive at work in the morning they 'hang up their personal values next to their coats'.

- People are invariably afflicted by 'workplace schizophrenia' – they feel they cannot bring 'their own self' to work.

- This psychological disjunction can only be overcome if the company as a whole transforms itself: 'Personal integrity cannot flourish outside a context of corporate integrity.'

This corporate integrity, in turn, can only be built by the right kind of leadership, one shaped by healthy emotional drivers. Steare identifies five key qualities:[8]

Principled leaders:

- display personal humility rather than ego

- are ambitious for the organisation rather than for themselves

- stand up for what they believe in with courage and fortitude

- make sure people with the right character are hired

- nurture core values – what can be defined as 'integrity'

Such ideas cannot be realised with small steps. Developing this new ethos of leadership calls for nothing less than a tectonic shift in how we think about business. The starting point for achieving this mind shift is understanding how corporations have evolved and the nature of the psychological contract they forged with the societies that spawned them – a contract based largely on mistrust and a license to exploit. That psychological contract is now due for fundamental revision.

The rise of the modern business corporation can be likened to Europe's colonial empires. Those empires grew, on a global scale, without rules and with a buccaneering disdain for the sensitivities of the people and territories they desired to conquer. They pushed back frontiers and overwhelmed local cultures, either destroying them or absorbing them into their own alien sphere. They fought each other over land, resources and markets. They merged with, conspired against and acquired one another. They expressed their values of superiority and civilising zeal through a host of imperial trappings – flags, anthems, uniforms, ceremonials, statues and grand buildings. Those empires created many heroes but also many myths. To echo terminology that lies at the centre of this book's analysis, those colonial empires were built on *aggression*, *arrogance* and sometimes *courage*. But in the end, as times changed, they crumbled.

For the most part those empires crumbled because the people they ruled would not buy the brand any more. As political consumers, their tastes and preferences had changed and they no longer accepted the legitimacy or values of imperial power. Much the same challenge now confronts the corporate world. It is the contention of this book that in the years ahead consumers will increasingly demand a new and better deal from the companies they keep. The emperors of the boardroom, so to speak, will be stripped of their clothes, to reveal the stark realities beneath. *The Bullshit Factor* has been written in the hope of sparking a new debate – and taking one small, but important, step towards re-evaluating our relationship with the corporations that have come to rule our lives. An eminent philosopher coined the maxim: 'The truth shall set you free'. It is time to recognise that truth and business success – and personal integrity – can coexist.

SOURCES

Introduction

1. Kets de Vries, Manfred. *The Leadership Mystique: A User's Manual for the Human Enterprise,* Financial Times Prentice Hall, 2001.

2. Levinson, Harry. *Why The Behemoths Fell,* American Psychologist, May 1994, Vol 49, No 5.

3. Miller, Danny. *The Icarus Paradox: How Exceptional Companies Bring About Their Own Downfall,* HarperBusiness, New York, 1991.

4. Bridges, William. *The Character of Organisations: Using Personality Type in Organisation Development,* Davies Black, 2000.

5. Hare, Robert. *The Psychopathy Checklist-Revised,* Multi-Health Systems, Toronto, 2003.

6. Frankfurt, Harry G. *On Bullshit,* Princeton University Press, 2005.

A Pressure to Deceive

1. www.altria.com, speech of 15 March 2005.

2. Hobsbawm, Julia (ed). *Where The Truth Lies: Morality and Trust in PR and Journalism,* Atlantic Books, 2006.

3. Bakan, Joel. *The Corporation: The Pathological Pursuit of Profit and Power,* Constable and Robinson, 2005.

4. Klein, Naomi. *No Logo: Taking Aim at the Brand Bullies,* Vintage Canada, 2000.

5. Day, Martin. Editor of *CAD Server,* 15 July 2002.

6. Strunk, William I and White, E. B. *The Elements of Style,* Longman, 1999.

7. Gilbreth, Lillian. *Psychology of Management,* The Thoemmes Libraries, 2003.

8. Drucker, Peter F. *Concept of the Corporation,* Transaction Publishers, US, 1996.

9. Carr, A Z. *Is Business Bluffing Ethical?* in *Harvard Business Review*, January 1968.

Greater than Empires

1. Brown, Bruce. *The History of the Corporation*, BF Communications Inc., 2003.

2. Matlack, Carol, Symonds, William and others. *The Vatican: Challenges Ahead, BusinessWeek* online, 18 April 2005; www. businessweek.com.

3. *The Guardian*, 25 June 2001.

4. Pool, James. *Who Financed Hitler?* Simon and Schuster, 1999.

5. *Harvard Business Review*, May 1994.

6. *BBC News Online*, 28 April 1999; www.bbc.co.uk.

7. Page, Martin, *The Company Savage*, Cassell & Co, 1972.

8. Hampden-Turner, Charles and Trompenaars, Fons. *The Seven Cultures of Capitalism*, Piatkus Books, 1994.

9. Levinson, *op cit.*

10. Hampden-Turner and Trompenaars, *op cit*, p116.

11. Kahn, Herman. *The Emerging Japanese Superstate: Challenge and response*, Deutsch, 1971.

12. Benedict, Ruth. *The Chrysanthemum and the Sword: Patterns of Japanese Culture*, Mariner Books, 2006.

13. Dore, R. P. *The Japanese Personality*, in Wint, Guy (ed). *Asia Handbook*, Penguin, 1969.

14. Eijiro, Inatomi. *The Japanese Mind: Essentials of Japanese Philosophy and Culture*, Moore, Charles A. (ed). East-West Center Press, Honolulu, 1967.

15. Kahn, *op cit*, p40.

16. *ibid*, p56.

17. Lashinsky, Adam. *Saving Face at Sony*, in *Fortune*, 21 February 2005.

18. *ibid.*

19. Onishi, Norimitsu. *Ugly Images of Asian Rivals Become Best Sellers in Japan*, in *The New York Times*, 19 November 2005.

20. Hampden-Turner and Trompenaars, *op cit.*

Where are the Corporate Good Guys?

1. Page, *op cit*, p41.

2. Bakan, *op cit*, pp18-19.

3. Jensen, Rolf. *The Dream Society: How The Coming Shift from Information to Imagination Will Transform Your Business*, McGraw-Hill Education, 2001.

4. Argenti, John. *Corporate Collapse: The Causes and Symptoms*, McGraw-Hill, 1976, p71.

5. Nader, Ralph. *Unsafe At Any Speed*, Knightsbridge Publishing Company, Mass., 1991.

6. Quoted in *Critics Fault Exxon* in *Christian Science Monitor*, 14 June 1989.

7. Steiner, Rick and Ott, Riki. *The Truth About The Exxon Valdez Oil Spill*, 16 November 1993. Also see Ott, Riki. *Sound Truth & Corporate Myth$: The Legacy of the Exxon Valdez Oil Spill*, Dragonfly Sisters Press, 2005.

8. Zarembo, Alan. *Exxon Funded Research Into Jury Awards* in *Washington Post*, 26 December 2003.

9. *Briefing For Ministers*, UN Climate Change Secretariat.

10. Several sources. For example, www.greenpeace.org; www.stoppesso.com.

11. *The Independent Online*, 25 August 2005.

12. info@clintonglobalinitiative.org.

13. *The Independent Online*, 3 July 2005.

14. www.shell.com/home.

15. http://archive.greenpeace.org/comms/brent/mar26.html.

16. *Failing The Challenge: The Other Shell Report,* Friends of the Earth, London 2003.

17. *ibid*, p24.

18. *World Cancer Report*, WHO, Geneva, 3 April 2003.

19. Freedman, Alix M. *Philip Morris Memo Likens Nicotine to Cocaine* in *The Wall Street Journal*, 5 December 1995.

20. Miles, Robert H. *Coffin Nails and Corporate Strategies*, Prentice Hall, 1982, p60.

21. Jim Hagart's Subliminal World at www.subliminalworld.org.

22. Savage, Jessica. *The Implications of Smoking Hazards on* (sic) *Cigarette Advertising,* at www.courses.rochester.edu.

23. Freedman, *op cit*; Freedman, Alix M. *Impact Booster: Tobacco Firm Shows How Ammonia Spurs Delivery of Nicotine* in *The Wall Street Journal*, 28 December 1995.

24. www.altria.com 2005.

25. *Our Agenda*, Body Shop publication, 1996.

26. Entine, Jon. *The Stranger-than-Truth Story of the Body Shop* in Wallis, David (ed). *Killed: Great Journalism Too Hot To Print*, Nation Books, New York, 2004. See also Entine, Jon. *A Social and Environmental Audit of the Body Shop: Anita Roddick and The Question of Character,* at www.jonentine.com.

The Dishonesty Pandemic

1. Michaels, Ed, Handfield-Jones, Helen and Axelrod, Beth. *The War for Talent*, Harvard Business School Press, 2001.

2. *Enron: Virtual Company, Virtual Profits* in *Financial Times*, 3 February 2002.

3. Coffee, J. C. *A Theory of Corporate Scandals: Why The US and Europe Differ,* Working Paper 274, March 2005, The Centre for Law and Economic Studies, New York.

4. *What Price SOX?* in *Network Computing,* 17 March 2005.

Snakes and Ladders

1. *Financial Times,* 8 October 2001.

2. www.telegraph.co.uk, 25 September 2005.

3. *Fortune Global 500* for 2005.

4. Interview cited on www.CNN.com, 14 June 2004.

Three Faces of Courage

1. Byrnes, Jonathan. *The Age of Precision Markets,* Harvard Business School Working Knowledge, 4 April 2005; see http://hbswk.hbs. edu.

2. Kaikati, Andrew and Kaikati, Jack. *Stealth Marketing: How To Reach Consumers Surreptitiously,* in *The California Management Review,* Issue 46/4, Summer 2004.

3. Eichenwald, Kurt. *Even If Heads Roll, Mistrust Will Live On,* in *The New York Times,* 6 October 2002.

4. *ibid.*

5. Waddock, Sandra. *A Radical New Agenda for Business in Society,* see www2.bc.edu/~waddock.

6. Eichenwald, *op cit.*

7. *Integrity in Practice,* Financial Services Authority, UK, September 2003.

8. Steare, Roger. *Integrity Works* in *Argent,* Vol 3, Issue 5.

SUGGESTED READING

Bakan, Joel. *The Corporation: The Pathological Pursuit of Profit and Power,* Constable and Robinson, 2005.

Benedict, Ruth. *The Chrysanthemum and the Sword: Patterns of Japanese Culture,* Mariner Books, 2006.

Brown, Bruce. *The History of the Corporation,* BF Communications Inc., 2003.

Business Ethics: a quarterly journal on all aspects of corporate behaviour; www.business-ethics.com.

Coffee, J C. *A Theory of Corporate Scandals: Why The US and Europe Differ,* Working Paper 274, March 2005, The Centre for Law and Economic Studies, New York.

Entine, Jon. *The Stranger-than-Truth Story of the Body Shop* in Wallis, David (ed). *Killed: Great Journalism Too Hot To Print,* Nation Books, New York, 2004.

Frankfurt, Harry G. *On Bullshit,* Princeton University Press, 2005.

Fukuyama, Francis. *Trust: the Social Virtues and the Creation of Prosperity*, Hamish Hamilton, 1995.

Grove, Andrew S. *Only The Paranoid Survive,* Doubleday, 1996.

Hampden-Turner, Charles and Trompenaars, Fons. *The Seven Cultures of Capitalism,* Piatkus Books, 1994.

Hobsbawm, Julia (ed). *Where The Truth Lies: Morality and Trust in PR and Journalism,* Atlantic Books, 2006.

Integrity in Practice, Financial Services Authority, UK, September 2003.

Jensen, Rolf. *The Dream Society: How The Coming Shift from Information to Imagination Will Transform Your Business*, McGraw-Hill Education, 2001.

Johnson, Larry and Philips, Bob. *Absolute Honesty: Building a Corporate Culture That Values Straight Talk and Rewards Integrity*, Amacom, 2003.

Kets de Vries, Manfred. *The Leadership Mystique: A User's Manual for the Human Enterprise*, Financial Times Prentice Hall, 2001.

Klein, Naomi. *No Logo: Taking Aim at the Brand Bullies*, Vintage Canada, 2000.

Miller, Danny. *The Icarus Paradox: How Exceptional Companies Bring About Their Own Downfall*, HarperBusiness, New York, 1992.

Ott, Riki. *Sound Truth & Corporate Myth$: The Legacy of the Exxon Valdez Oil Spill*, Dragonfly Sisters Press, 2005.

Packard, Vance. *The Hidden Persuaders*, Penguin, 1957.

Page, Martin. *The Company Savage*, Cassell & Co, 1972.

Penny, Laura. *Your Call Is Important To Us: The Truth About Bullshit*, Crown Publishers, 2005.